The Duchess of Devonshire's
CHATSWORTH COOKERY BOOK

To the memory of Jean-Pierre Béraud
and all the Chatsworth cooks, past and present

The Duchess of Devonshire's
CHATSWORTH
COOKERY BOOK

THE DUCHESS OF DEVONSHIRE

with the help of the chefs at Chatsworth

Hervé Marchand

Darren Wright

Philip Gates

André Birkett

FRANCES LINCOLN

The initials **DD** denote the Duchess of Devonshire
The initials at the end of the recipes denote the cooks who provided them:
HM Hervé Marchand
DW Darren Wright
PG Philip Gates
AB André Birkett

NOTE Throughout this book both metric and imperial measurements
are given. Use either all metric or all imperial, as the two are not
necessarily interchangeable.
All vegetables should be peeled unless stated otherwise.

Frances Lincoln Limited
4 Torriano Mews
Torriano Avenue
London NW5 2RZ
www.franceslincoln.com

First Frances Lincoln edition 2003

British Library Cataloguing-in-Publication Data
A catalogue record for this book is available from the British Library
ISBN 0 7112 2257 6

Printed in Singapore
2 4 6 8 9 7 5 3 1

Contents

INTRODUCTION

I HAVEN'T COOKED SINCE THE WAR. I hoped this would be the title of this book, but it was not well looked on by others. However, it is true and I am all for truth.

I told my old friend, the hairdresser from Chesterfield, that in spite of this lack of practical experience I planned to write a cookery book. He told his wife. 'Well,' she said, 'that's rich. It's like a blind woman driving down the M1.'

It is in response to our visitors who, surprised and intrigued to discover that this enormous house is lived in by a family, want to know more about everyday life here, and especially about the kitchen and the food that comes out of it – what's for lunch, is there tea, and is dinner a grand affair for twenty people or is it vegetable soup and an egg? – that I have tried to answer the kitchen question. Being greedy, I have done so with great pleasure. Anticipation of something delicious is a vital part of my day and the realisation is better still. That is why I have collected the receipts of my favourites between these covers. (The word receipt has the same meaning as recipe. I have grown up with the former. It is old-fashioned now and makes my grandchildren laugh like other words and pronunciations which are only used by the very old.)

I am lucky to live surrounded by cooks and purveyors of food. People who come to Chatsworth want to be fed and they all want something different from the food they cook in their own kitchens. While our friends and relations stay with us, some visitors go to the restaurant in the Carriage House, and others go to the Farm Shop Pantry.

This feeding is comparatively new. All a visitor used to find in the way of refreshment here was a single tap from which flowed cold water. Now this tap has a bucket underneath and carries a notice: 'WATER FOR DOGS'. In 1975 a basic 'tea bar' was rigged up in some stalls in the stables. This unpleasant arrangement was followed four years later by a scarcely better café, and it was not until 1991 that we tackled the problem and opened the Carriage House Restaurant. It is managed by Philip Gates, Head of Catering, who has a flair for food and has made a huge success of this important job. His kitchen, which serves the restaurant and Jean-Pierre's Bar (opened in 1997), now feeds more than 20,000 people every month when the house and garden are open.

As well as daily bread for our visitors Philip often lays on a special dinner for up to 250 people. Cooking on such a scale and to time, serving three courses quickly – we've all suffered the endless waits between courses at 'public' dinners with food of mediocre quality at best, uneatable at worst – is, to me, in the nature of a miracle. So, for people who from time to time find themselves faced with having to provide lunch or dinner for larger numbers than usual, Philip has provided some receipts of dishes that can be cooked at home and are as good for ten people as for fifty or even a hundred.

The Farm Shop, which opened in 1977, sells beef, lamb and venison direct to the customer from the in-hand Chatsworth Farm and estate farming tenants. Game from the surrounding land is available as well as potatoes from our Elm Tree Farm at Stoney Houghton, twenty miles to the east. The shop provides much else – pork, hams, sausages, bread, cakes, biscuits, fruit, vegetables, dairy products, preserves, honey and lovely chocolates made in the old station yard at Bakewell – and the delicatessen counter offers all sorts of best this and super that including vegetarian food plus more than thirty-five different British cheeses. We aim for the Best of British and we think it comes from round here.

Hervé Marchand and Darren Wright in our kitchen.
The table was in use in the 1820s.

My father-in-law's Jersey cows used to stand where the ovens and mixing machines of the Farm Shop kitchen are now. Butchers make tonnes of twelve different kinds of sausages. Bakers and cooks make all the bread, cakes, puddings, pies and pâtés which supply an avalanche of customers and fill the Christmas hampers. They cook for the Farm Shop Pantry, a fifty-six-seater restaurant attached, where you can read the paper over breakfast, follow it with a lunch of a hot roast and a really good pudding and then enjoy a hefty tea according to the English taste. André Birkett is in charge of the Farm Shop kitchen. His enthusiasm, business sense and deep interest in all that goes on there have been a big factor in its success. He has provided receipts for items that are particularly popular in the shop.

More chefs of high repute work in our two hotels in Yorkshire – the Devonshire Arms Country House Hotel, at Bolton Abbey, near Ilkley, awarded a Michelin star in 2003, and the Devonshire Fell at Burnsall, six miles higher up beautiful Wharfedale. Altogether, from farm to plate, 331 people are employed in the food and catering business by the Trustees of the Chatsworth Settlement.

Surrounded by all these professional experts, our own kitchen is a comparatively small affair in numbers, but it is of first importance to me. Hervé Marchand runs it with immense skill and dedication, ably assisted by Darren Wright.

Hervé has to cope with unsocial hours – late dinners and early breakfasts – and extremes of few and many for meals. We go along quietly for days on end with lunch and simple supper and then suddenly – for instance during the cricket weekend for my grandson's team and their wives and girlfriends – there is a crowd for breakfast, lunch, tea and dinner. Christmas is the busiest time of all, when there is no let-up and meals seem to run into each other – a challenge for all concerned. On top of everything else, there is the Christmas tree tea party for the children of those who work here and of Pilsley School. Last year ninety-nine children came – a record number.

Our food is served in the earthenware dishes seen in every French market or white French porcelain dishes, all from Divertimenti. Once in a blue moon huge silver dishes come out of the safe. The advantage of these is that they don't break and they do look good on a grand occasion. But for everyday it's back to basics and earthenware.

It is the same for the food – nothing fancy is the usual story, with stops pulled out once in a while. This country produces some of the best ingredients in the world, and it is up to us to use them to advantage. Hervé understands that this is the key to our enjoyment of his art. The result is straightforward cooking – with little or no decoration – that does not disguise the basic components. He is educated in food like a university professor and because he does not work within the time constraints that most home cooks have to face, he makes the best use of his knowledge in the classic way, taking no short cuts. In the receipts of his that are included here, his methods may seem lengthy and the number of ingredients inordinate, but both reflect his aim to make the most of everything. Hervé's is the very opposite of fast food.

Seasonal food is part of the pleasure of eating, to my mind. Now that asparagus and strawberries come from the ends of the earth and are for sale twelve months of the year, gone is the excitement of the first English asparagus, which belongs to May, as strawberries do to June. That is when the taste is there. Out-of-season food looks the same as the real stuff but after one bite you realise that it is altogether different and not to be bothered with. The freezer is also a culprit. It is a blessing 90 per cent of the time, but it is also guilty of providing game in May or raspberries in January. No, thanks.

Andrew (Cavendish) and I were married in 1941. He is easy to feed, thank goodness, and over the years has seldom complained about what is put before him. His Devonshire grandmother (or rather her cooks based at Chatsworth) left boxes full of papers with the menus for banquets at Government House in Ottawa (the 9th Duke was Governor-General of Canada 1916–21), dinners at their London home, Devonshire House,

Piccadilly, picnic lunches at Bolton Abbey, in Yorkshire, another of their several houses, where they spent every August, Christmas tea parties for children, as well as the day-to-day fare of a big house, including dining room, school room and nursery meals here at Chatsworth. The Chatsworth Household Accounts are mighty volumes. The itemised lots are written in the exquisite script learned by the clerks when at Edensor School (boys only, who were beaten for walking on the grass).

My own family – and I am no exception – have always been interested in feeding their guests (and themselves) and I have inherited receipts from my mother and from my sisters Nancy, Pam and Diana. My mother kept her household accounts in narrow leather-bound books. She did so from an early age, as her own mother died when she was eight and she soon found herself keeping house for her father and her younger brothers and sister. Every penny spent, every item bought was recorded in her round handwriting, a discipline she continued after she married and had her own family.

In 1918 she noted the quantities for tea for 1,000 people at Batsford Park, then our home at Moreton-in-Marsh, thus:

2000 small cakes	8·18·0	
20 lb large cakes	1-16-8	
16 gall milk at 1/10	1-9-4	12 quarts to 100 persons
10 lb tea at 2/8	1-6-8	1 lb to 100
30 lb butter at 2/6	3-15-0	3 lb to 100
50 quarterns bread	1-17-6	4 quarterns to 100
	19-3-2	Cost of tea for 1,000 persons – or 5d each

An afterthought was 'Sugar 130 lumps to 1 lb', but she forgot to write down the price – a rare lapse, because she was very aware that there is no such thing as a free lump of sugar.

A small fat notebook, 4 x 2½in, has a dark red cover and on it in blue ink, almost invisible now, is written 'Dances 27 May 1930–30 March 1939'.

The first was for my brother Tom's coming of age. She lists the names of those dining at our house in Rutland Gate on that occasion: Mrs Winston Churchill gave a dinner and so did my sister Diana, who had married Bryan Guinness the year before. Diana was not yet twenty. The list of young men she invited reads like a taste of things to come: Mr Henry Yorke (the novelist Henry Green), Mr Eddie Marsh, Mr Armstrong-Jones, Mr Harold Acton, Mr Roy Harrod, Mr John Betjeman, Mr Lytton Strachey – not exactly deb's delights.

In those days the hostess of a dance asked friends to give dinners for the young people so that they could meet each other before going on to the dance, which began at 10 or 10.30 p.m. The idea was that the young men should ask the girls sitting on either side of them at dinner for the first two dances. In my experience this seldom happened and the men bolted as soon as they could, to find a more attractive partner. Supper was provided at the dance at around midnight. This was usually a substantial affair, arranged, I suppose, for those not included in dinner parties, but all made their way to the supper room and the food was an important part of the night's entertainment for the unfortunate chaperones. It was the custom for the mothers (and, rarely, the fathers) of the debutantes to go to the dance and sit on one of the hired gilt chairs that surrounded the dance floor, till the daughter had had enough and wanted to go home. My dutiful mother suffered this extraordinary fate for six seasons, one for each daughter. At 10 p.m. on four or five nights a week in May, June and July she looked longingly at her turned-down bed, put on an evening dress and set off alone for the party. For those like her of the older generation, supper was a pleasant interlude Once in a while my father gave my mother a night off and was the unwilling guest at a dance. He made no pretence of enjoying it, but sat in the hall, hands folded on the handle of his stick and his black cape on his shoulders, waiting for the blessed moment of retreat. I remember a worried hostess, hearing of his lone vigil, dashing to the hall. 'Lord Redesdale, would you like some supper?' 'NO,' my father bellowed. 'I'd like to be left in peace.'

Marcel Boulestin, master chef and proprietor of the best restaurant near Covent Garden Opera House, was a friend of my aunt's and it seems that my mother used this distinguished man as if his restaurant was any old takeaway. He provided the dinner and the supper for Tom's dance. Under 'Boulestin' she notes:

Duck au Chambertin for 30	£8-0-0
Potatoes	£1-10-0
Fraises des bois au champagne	£3-0-0

The supper dishes included 12 lb of caviar ('8 or 9 would have been plenty', she noted) at £2-8-0 per pound. The total cost of food for thirty for dinner and ninety for supper was £48-15-0. '£40 would have been amply enough' was her comment.

Iced coffee, 10 quarts, came from Gunter's, the famous tea-shop in Curzon Street, and cost £2-10-0. Add lager beer, champagne (Binet 1921 at £4-19-6 per dozen), one bottle of brandy and one bottle of port – and the drinks came to £26-17-0. The Embassy band, four performers, played from 10 p.m. to 3 a.m. for £31-10-0. The final figure for my brother's coming-of-age party in 1930 was £134-13-10. About 125 people came, so the whole evening's entertainment cost just over £1 per head.

My mother's father, Thomas Gibson Bowles, one-time MP for King's Lynn, had strong views on health and food, as he had on everything else. 'I will not have my meat in a puddle,' he used to shout. 'Very little of very good' was his maxim, with which I heartily agree. He brought up my mother and her three siblings according to the laws of Moses when it came to food. Only meat from animals which divide the hoof and chew the cud was allowed and fish had to have scales and fins, so they never ate pig, rabbit, hare or shellfish. My mother tried to keep her own children on this straight and narrow path (very wise, no doubt, in the Holy Land before the advent of refrigerators, but hardly necessary in Oxfordshire in the twentieth century). It gave us a longing for sausages, ham, bacon and lobster which has remained with me.

Pig meat was provided for my father, so the longed-for sausages were on the hot plate at breakfast and sometimes a sugar-glazed ham appeared – for him, but not for us. Mabel in the pantry was our friend and occasionally she allowed us the congealing remains after my father had left the dining room. (He took his last cup of coffee – 'my suckments', he called it – with him to his business room, and put it in the safe in case someone tried to clear it away.)

But even without this forbidden fruit, my mother's food was original and it was excellent. Several of her receipts, tried, tasted and trusted over the years, appear in this book.

My sisters inherited my mother's talent for housekeeping in varying degrees. My eldest sister, Nancy, could not, and never tried to, boil a kettle, but lunch or dinner in her house never disappointed especially after she went to live in Paris. Her friend Gaston Palewski (Fabrice in her novel *The Pursuit of Love*) was very fond of English puddings – apple crumble, treacle tart and the other classics. She used to moan about the difficulty of explaining to her cook Marie how to make these foreign concoctions. Always in a hurry, Gaston would rush in for lunch at her flat in the rue Monsieur, only to dash out again as soon as he had eaten. A good pudding held him a little longer. She herself was no good at cooking. During the war she was staying with my father, who had been ill and had eaten nothing. He suddenly fancied an egg, so, pleased to be of help, she boiled some water and threw in an egg. She was dismayed when, as she put it, a sinister sort of octopus grew out of it. So she threw in two more – the whole week's ration – and the same thing happened. Then she gave up.

Pam, born three years after Nancy, was a real cook, with an exceptional talent for making everything taste good. Food was important to her and so was her kitchen garden. She was a careful shopper and spent a lot of time talking to the butcher or fishmonger (not the baker – she made her own bread). In the long-lost days of Bath Chaps my father introduced her to surprised strangers as, 'This is my daughter Pamela, the best judge of a pig's face in the south of England.' She once went to a smart lunch party in Paris where she sat next to Charles de Noailles, then the acknowledged arbiter of elegance. She explained to him the glories of some special cut of pork and, carried away by enthusiasm, and to the astonishment of the company, she stood up, slapped her thigh and said, 'Il faut le coupé *là*.'

We used to say she remembered what she had eaten at every lunch since 1931. It was nearly true. She loved experimenting with new dishes, putting her own stamp and taste into them. When she was married to the charming, eccentric and brilliant Derek Jackson, spectroscopist, National Hunt amateur rider who rode in several Grand Nationals and gallant wartime RAF officer, they had a series of cooks. Pam's relationship with whoever was in her kitchen was uneasy as she was too critical, knowing that she could have done it better herself.

Diana was the fourth of the family, born in 1910. Her house has always been perfect in my eyes and in the eyes of those lucky enough to go there. She married when she was eighteen and at ninety-three keeps up the standard she has, perhaps unconsciously, set herself. Long before cooking was a subject of great moment and cooks became stars of the television screen, she valued them and their work, discussing, praising and encouraging. Whoever works in her kitchen is appreciated, and his or her talent flourishes to the intense pleasure of her guests.

When Diana and her second husband, Sir Oswald Mosley, lived at Le Temple de la Gloire in Orsay, seventeen miles south-west of Paris, every meal was perfection. Emmie Lehane, born in Co. Galway, and her husband Jerry, friend/butler/chauffeur to my brother-in-law for forty years, were the reasons. Emmie produced feasts, for as many as ten people, out of a kitchen the size of a sixpence. Her chicken, or sometimes veal, cooked with chicory, mushrooms, onions and a few olives was the best ever. Emmie Lehane's talent as a cook was on a par with Kathleen Penny's at Lismore Castle, our house in Co. Waterford where we spent nearly fifty Aprils from 1947. There must be something in the Irish air which inspired these two remarkable women.

Unity was born in 1914. She did not marry and died when she was only thirty-four. Where food was concerned, she loved her fancy of the moment, and chose to live on mashed potatoes laced with butter, cream and milk for a year or two in childhood. My mother was understanding of this, in the same way that she allowed me to eat bread sauce, a passion of mine, and little else for a time. Bread sauce is, after all, only bread and milk made savoury. We were never forced to eat food we didn't like, for which I was thankful, and we were allowed to choose, even if the choice was sometimes considered to be eccentric.

The next sister to me was Jessica, always called Decca. She lived in Oakland, California, with her second husband, Bob Treuhaft, and her family. She enjoyed cooking for parties, but the everyday slog did not appeal. Some of her letters to me describing food are brilliantly illustrated. One shows a salmon and Decca looking at each other in surprise before she cooked it for some special occasion. When the Parent Teacher Association of her children's school asked for a contribution to their cookery book, she wrote, 'Roast goose. Take a goose and roast it till done.' History does not relate if she recommended plucking it first. Nevertheless, this refreshingly simple receipt was included in the book.

Andrew's family was different from ours, in that their various kitchens were far-away places, another land where children were not welcome. It was no good the Cavendish boys dashing down the endless passages to beg a square of cooking chocolate, as we did when I was a child at Asthall and Swinbrook. The pantry was their haven; the butler and footmen were their friends rather than the cook. Andrew's grandparents' cook at Chatsworth, Mrs Tanner, who trained under Escoffier in Paris, was renowned, but her efforts at producing wonderful dishes must have been hampered by the distance they had to travel before they reached the dining-room table. In spite of running footmen and a series of hot cupboards next to the dining room, it was a physical impossibility to succeed with anything that had to be 'served immediately'.

After Mrs Tanner, and her daughter Maud who followed her as cook, Granny lost interest in food and some of the nastiest meals I have ever eaten were under her roof after she was widowed and lived at Hardwick Hall. One of her grandsons, who was staying with her, escaped in despair and came across the hills to us. The last straw for him was barley pudding, from which the barley water had already been made. Granny seemed to enjoy the wartime and post-war shortages and would gladly have lived on nettle soup with a dandelion leaf here and there for the rest of her life.

But between the wars when Chatsworth was going full blast she had to entertain on the sort of scale expected. A menu from Mrs Tanner's reign, dated 4 July 1933, has survived. King George V and Queen Mary stayed for the Royal Show held at Derby that year and this is what they ate for dinner one night: Crème Sarah Bernhardt, Barbue Grimaldi, Caneton à l'Anglaise, Poussin Rôtis, Legumes, Mousse de Jambon, Salade Waldorf, Soufflé Esterhazy, Fraises Romanoff, Chester Cakes. The number of courses was typical for a formal dinner at that time – a feat of organisation by the kitchen staff. Imagine eating all that, and the time it must have taken to serve so many courses. And then consider the washing up ....

In the 1920s and 1930s the kitchen staff at Chatsworth consisted of the cook, a first and second kitchen maid, a vegetable maid and two or three scullery maids. Two stillroom maids and a dairy maid completed the women whose work was with food. They were not allowed to speak to the eleven housemaids nor, of course, to the army of menservants. Such rules were made to be broken and broken they often were. The cook was responsible for her girls and was, of necessity, a disciplinarian. Her word was law over her staff.

The first kitchen maid cooked for the school room and nursery, the second kitchen maid cooked for the servants. The vegetable maid prepared the vegetables for the family. She did her own washing up. The scullery maids prepared the vegetables for the servants and washed up for the cook and kitchen maids. They had 'a man' to clean the coppers.

The dairy maid received the milk and eggs from the farm and was responsible for issuing these to the kitchen and stillroom and milk to the housemaids' room, the laundry maids and the servants' hall. In spring she pickled surplus eggs in huge pottery jars filled with brine. She made the butter and helped the stillroom maids at busy times, and cooked for the Duke if he stayed at Chatsworth alone while the Duchess and the rest of the household were elsewhere.

Dining room, school room and nursery all had different menus in the days when Andrew's aunts were children. The poor things had to eat the hateful bland food thought suitable for their ages. Even the Christmas puddings were made of different ingredients according to where they would be eaten. Those for the staff were mostly suet and breadcrumbs mixed with stout and milk, whereas Mrs Tanner's 'Best Christmas Pudding – Buckingham Palace receipt' included French plums, stoned raisins and half muscatels, plus half a bottle of brandy.

A slip of paper headed 'Lord Charles's Wedding Lunch' reveals a sign of economy as far back as 1932. On 9 May that year Charlie Cavendish, Andrew's uncle, married Adele Astaire, Fred's sister, in the chapel at Chatsworth. Mrs Tanner's suggestions for the festive occasion were 'Mayonnaise de Saumon, Poulet de grain [wheat-fed chicken] en casserole – Sauce Crème, Quartier d'Agneau rôti – Sauce menthe, legumes, Cold ham, Beef, Brawn, Tongue, Salades', ending with 'Éclairs au Chocolat'. 'French pastry' was crossed out by Granny and next to 'Compote of Mixed Fruits and Grapefruit Jelly', 'need not have both' is written in her hand. Perhaps the real reason for this parsimony was that she did not approve of her son's marriage.

The Devonshires' year was punctuated by moves to their other houses and August found them at Bolton Abbey for the grouse shooting. The picnic lunches there were famously good. The stoves were lit at 5 a.m. so the rolls could be baked and ready in time to be packed in the hampers which were taken up to the lunch huts on the moor by tractor. A tin box was ingeniously made, with its own china dishes fitting into tin shelves, to carry cold grouse from the previous day's shoot, ham, tongue and other cold meats, Cornish pasties, potato salad and a cold pudding, often treacle tart or something similar which would not spill, and a Stilton cheese. We still use this tin box. Coffee was the only hot item, brewed in the lunch hut in a sort of samovar, its flame fed by methylated spirits. The coffee usually suffered from being boiled, but at least it was hot.

Modern Thermos flasks make these picnics much easier now. It is a luxury to have a hot stew on those days when cold wind and stinging rain make fingers numb and turn eyes into slits.

I have never discovered how much Granny and Mrs Tanner saw of each other. I would love to know who took the long walk to whom – Granny to the kitchen or Mrs Tanner to the boudoir – to discuss the food, or if it was all done through Elsie Saunders, the loved secretary. Such domestic details are not recorded and suddenly everyone who would have known is dead and gone.

Mary Devonshire, my mother-in-law, did not have enough time to make her mark after her husband inherited Chatsworth in 1938. She planned an ingenious railway to bring the food from kitchen to dining room, but the 1939 war intervened. It would have been fascinating to know whether or not it would have worked.

When we moved in twenty years later, there was much switching of rooms to enable the house to be run on a smaller scale. The 1959 kitchen is the third to be made here, but it has links with the past in its massive kitchen table (illustrated in William Henry Hunt's watercolour of the Bachelor Duke's 1820s kitchen) and nineteenth-century copper utensils. It is a light and cheerful room with a view of the garden. Those who work there seem to like it.

*Philip Gates walking through the Carriage House Restaurant. Andrew and I went
to the Queen's Coronation in the nineteenth-century state coach on the balcony.*

There is something about working in a kitchen that produces 'characters' – like those chefs who crop up nightly on the telly. I don't know why they have to be so unpleasant, but that is the fashion now – something I couldn't put up with at such close quarters. The nearest thing we had to these despots was the mighty Mrs Canning (the double of Honoré de Balzac, according to Nancy and Diana, and I must say a portrait of him with straight black hair to below the ears and a rugby player's neck was Mrs Canning to the life). An enormous woman, she was a talented cook who demanded the highest standards from the girls who slaved under her. Before our annual August visit to Bolton Abbey she ordered a lorry to be loaded with sugar, being under the impression that you couldn't get it in Yorkshire. I kept out of her way in the days before the migration.

In 1978 a twenty-two-year-old Frenchman from a suburb of Paris arrived here by divine providence – the divine part given a shove by my sister Diana. For the next eighteen years Jean-Pierre Béraud made his home and his name here. He transformed our kitchen, saved the Farm Shop from closing (it was losing money) and started the Carriage House Restaurant in the stables. He married a beautiful wife, had two sons and was on the crest of the wave when he was killed in a motor accident, aged forty. A colleague who wrote to me on his death said, 'He was like a blazing comet in my life.' And so he was. He ruled an ever-growing empire with brilliance and authority and his influence on Chatsworth was incalculable.

Jean-Pierre left us a golden legacy in the people who worked with him. He had encouraged Sara Ridgway and then Michael Kokuciak, who kept our own food flag flying wonderfully well for years while he was busy with the Farm Shop and the Restaurant, and their efforts were greatly appreciated. No cross old cooks they, but young and cheerful and always a pleasure to be with. Philip Gates worked with Jean-Pierre for four years in the Carriage House Restaurant and André Birkett came as a student under Jean-Pierre in 1982. Hervé Marchand and Jean-Pierre

– both Frenchmen who chose to live in England – naturally gravitated towards each other and became friends through their passionate interest in food.

It has been of intense interest and pleasure to me to watch these wonderful people cook and to eat what they have made, and I fully realise my luck in having had them in our house. Over the years we all talked of 'doing a book' and, in their various ways, all have contributed to this one because many of our perennially favourite dishes have evolved through them. Other receipts are more recent introductions as tastes have changed.

According to Nancy, I can only read with the help of a pointing finger. She was about right, so my room is lined with books that suit my pitiful no-attention span. There are reference books and books by my grandfathers, sisters, children, nephews, cousins and friends, old and new. And now that some of these have become famous there are books about them too. You can't escape advice on goat-keeping and poultry-keeping, biographies of Elvis and the shelves marked 'FOOD'. These are full of enormous books with course after course brightly illustrated by full-page photographs of dishes arranged by a new breed of people called stylists. I find myself flipping through them as I do expensive art-books, but they are somehow not serious.

My favourite cookery books, which are neither big, nor do they have coloured illustrations, are two by a distant cousin, Dorothy Alhusen: *A Book of Scents and Dishes*, 1925, and *A Medley of Recipes*, 1936. I never met the author, but her books have an added interest because it was when staying in her house in 1936 that my sister Decca met Esmond Romilly. Kindred revolutionary spirits, they fell instantly in love, ran away to 'fight' in the Spanish Civil War on the side of the Communists, were married soon after, and were only separated by his death in 1942 when he was serving in the Canadian Air Force.

I like Mrs Alhusen's style: 'take some'; 'boil the tongue in the usual way'; 'very little'; 'plenty'; 'put just as many pears as look nice in the dish'; and I appreciate advice such as how to prevent butter from tasting of turnips. In the twenty-first century this paragraph would fall on deaf ears, but was very relevant in the days when herds and the dairies they supplied were small enough for the diet of the cows to be of great importance. The milk used for the butter would be called 'traceable' now, traceable by the taste of turnips. Another pleasing item is 'Sprouts Made Edible' – just add half their weight of chestnuts. Easy.

Mrs Alhusen's receipts are gathered from friends and relations, from chefs of favoured restaurants, including some extravagances from the Ritz Hotel, as well as some from some seemingly unlikely contributors – Mrs Thomas Hardy, Mrs Edith Wharton and Mrs John Galsworthy. Also quoted are Lady Blanche Hozier and her daughters, Mrs Winston Churchill and Mrs Romilly (Esmond's mother).

Lady Blanche lived in Dieppe for the sake of economy. She terrorised the local children (and grown-ups) by emptying the slops from a first-floor window of her house on any passers-by she did not like, and she disliked a great many people. Aunt Natty, as my parents called her, was born Ogilvy and was indeed my father's aunt. A great gambler, she was always on the verge of going broke. Nevertheless, her food was as famously good as her love life was indiscriminate. The paternity of her daughter Clementine Churchill is still the subject of discussion. At one time Aunt Natty lived in London and my mother told me that she used to walk round Eaton Square dressed in her nightgown followed by a pet hen on a lead. No one would be surprised by the nightgown now – half London seems to walk the streets in such garments – but, a hundred years ago, the combination of the hen and her clothes surprised her more conventional neighbours.

Mrs Alhusen's books make compulsive reading, but they were written as reminders for employers of experienced cooks and some of the guesswork directions are vague. On the assumption that the Dear

Reader of this book is not a trained cook, exact quantities and clear instructions are given for all the receipts it contains in the hopes of Avoiding Disappointment.

The distilled kitchen wisdom of my mother, other relations and friends, and the contents of a box of yellowing bits of paper – that, with Hervé's, Philip's and André's contributions, make up this collection – have all been tried and noted by Hervé, and eaten by our guests and us.

We know that one man's meat is another man's poison, but trusting that this collection is not altogether poisonous, we hope that you may find something in it which pleases.

Deborah Devonshire

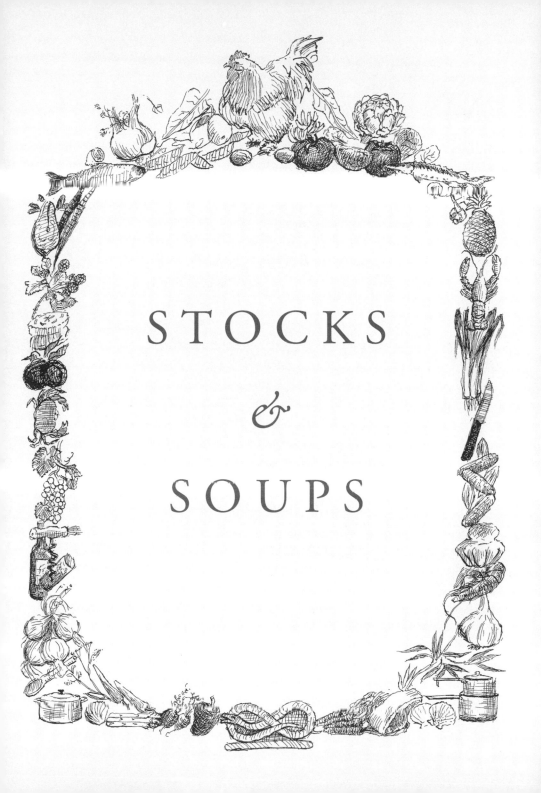

STOCKS

&

SOUPS

M AKING STOCK IS A TROUBLE, but worth it because it freezes well and can pause in the freezer till something special is needed and then – taste the difference. At Lismore I asked Kathleen Penny (an inspired cook who makes our visits to Ireland a fattening time) how she makes her superb consommé. 'Oh, all the bits', she said cheerfully, leaving me none the wiser. The easiest of Hervé's stocks, and the base for many sauces as well as soups, is the versatile white chicken stock.

In days gone by all poultry ended up as bones simmering in a pot as a matter of course. The very idea of throwing away a chicken carcass or burying old hens whose laying days were done would have shocked the older generation, who would have thought it a wicked waste of valuable food. I once had a very bad-tempered Light Sussex cock which flew at people claws first and made a nasty mess of their legs. My father wrung his neck and he was sent in a jelly (the cock, not my father) to an ill person who lived near by. The cross creature had simply been turned into the best stock.

My sister Pam was the queen of soup. 'How do you make it?' I used to ask, when something wonderful appeared from nowhere. 'Oh, out of my head', she used to say. I bitterly regret not asking her which bit of her head it was made from and watching her do it. No feast in a grand restaurant could be better than one of her soups with a hunk of home-made bread to go with it.

She grew vegetables in her high Cotswold garden, preferring them to flowers. Among her favourites was sorrel, which deserves a place in all gardens, because it is seldom seen in shops. Pam's original plants came from France, given her by Robin Adair, a great cook who was a protégé of the chef Marcel Boulestin. She took roots of this sorrel (the advantage of the French kind of *Rumex acetosa* is that is does not 'bolt' or run to seed) to plant wherever she was living and we have it in the garden here. Its clean and slightly bitter taste is unique – valued in salad or giving an extra zip to cooked spinach – and it is an essential ingredient of Hervé's Germiny soup. DD

WHITE CHICKEN STOCK

This is very versatile – useful for soups, cream sauces, blanquettes, white stews and for braising vegetables, and we always have a supply in the freezer. No salt is added so that it can be reduced to your liking when making sauces.

MAKES 3.5 LITRES/6 PINTS

2.7kg/6lb fresh chicken bones/
   carcass, with the skin and the
   'parson's nose' (which hides a gland
   with a bitter taste) removed
350g/12oz onions, cut in half
200g/7oz celery
350g/12oz clean leek trimmings (use
   only the outer parts and keep the
   best for other uses)
225g/8oz carrots

3 garlic cloves
150g/5oz white mushrooms
30g/1oz parsley
2 bay leaves
2 sprigs fresh, or 1 teaspoon dried,
   thyme
1 tablespoon black peppercorns
3 cloves
juice of 1 lemon

Put the chicken bones in a pan and cover them with cold water (about 6.75l/12 pints). Bring to the boil, and skim off all impurities and fat that rise to the surface. Add all the vegetables, which can be cooked whole, the herbs, spices and lemon juice and simmer for 1½ hours, skimming regularly. Take off the heat and lift out the bones, vegetables and herbs and discard them. Strain the stock through a fine mesh sieve into a clean pan. There should be about 4.5l/8 pints. Boil to reduce the quantity and concentrate the flavour until there are about 3.5l/6 pints left. Cool, and either refrigerate and use within 3 days, or freeze.

You can reduce the stock further so that it is less bulky to store, and then dilute it to the required concentration when needed. **HM**

BROWN CHICKEN STOCK

This stock differs from the white in that it is given colour and flavour by roasting the bones before they are simmered with vegetables. It is also reduced to a greater concentration than the white stock, which makes it an ideal base for gravies and brown sauces, as well as for meat stews.

MAKES 1.5 LITRES/2½ PINTS OF CONCENTRATED STOCK

2.7kg/6lb fresh chicken bones/carcass, with the skin and the 'parson's nose' (which hides a gland with a bitter taste) removed

2 tablespoons vegetable oil

275ml/½ pint dry white wine

1 large onion, top and tail removed, skin left on, cut into 3 slices horizontally

225g/8oz onions, cut in half

175g/6oz celery

225g/8oz carrots

175g/6oz clean leek trimmings (use only the outer parts and keep the best for other uses)

200g/7oz tinned chopped tomatoes in tomato juice

150g/5oz mushrooms

3 garlic cloves

30g/1oz parsley

2 bay leaves

2 sprigs fresh, or 1 teaspoon dried, thyme

1 tablespoon black peppercorns

Preheat the oven to 180C/350F/Gas 4. Place the bones in a roasting tray, drizzle over the oil, turning the bones to coat them with the oil, and roast for ¾–1 hour, turning the bones after 20 minutes so they brown evenly. Transfer the bones into a stockpot. Reheat the roasting tray on the top of the stove, pour off the fat and add the white wine. Bring this to the boil for a minute or two to reduce the acidity of the wine, and then scrape all the contents of the tray into the stockpot. Cover the bones with cold water (about 6.75l/12 pints) and bring to the boil. Skim off any impurities and fat that rise to the surface. Add the prepared vegetables and herbs and peppercorns, and simmer for 1½ hours, skimming regularly.

Take off the heat, lift out the bones, vegetables and herbs and discard them. Strain the stock through a fine mesh sieve into a clean pan. There should be about 4.5l/8 pints. Boil the stock to reduce the quantity and concentrate the flavour, reducing it to about 3.5l/6 pints to use as the base for brown soups or stews, or to about 1.5l/2½ pints for a darker, more concentrated chicken syrup for sauces and gravies. Cool, and either refrigerate and use within 3 days, or freeze. HM

FISH STOCK

MAKES 1 LITRE/1¾ PINTS

40g/1½oz butter
1 onion, finely sliced
2 shallots, finely sliced
2 leeks (white part only), split lengthways, washed and finely sliced
½ celery stick, finely sliced
110g/4oz white mushrooms

700 g/1lb 8oz bones from white flesh fish, chopped
330ml/12fl oz dry white wine
12 white peppercorns
25g/1oz parsley
1 bay leaf
2 sprigs fresh, or 1 teaspoon dried, thyme
juice of 1 lemon

Melt the butter over a medium heat. Add the vegetables with half a cup of water and cook without letting them colour for a few minutes to soften them. Add the fish bones and wine. Bring to the boil for a minute or two to reduce the acidity of the wine. Then add 850ml/1½ pints of water, the peppercorns, herbs and lemon juice and return to the boil. Skim off any impurities that rise to the surface. Lower the heat and simmer for about 20 minutes. Strain through a fine mesh sieve, pressing down lightly to extract all the liquid, into a clean pan. Bring to the boil and reduce to about 1l/1¾ pints. Cool, and either refrigerate and use within 3 days, or freeze. HM

VEGETABLE STOCK

MAKES 1.2 LITRES/2 PINTS

2 medium onions, chopped

4 celery sticks, cut into
  1cm/½in pieces

2 small leeks, cut into
  1cm/½in pieces

5 medium carrots, cut into
  1cm/½in pieces

1 fennel bulb, cut into
  1cm/½in pieces

12 garlic cloves

10 white peppercorns

5 black peppercorns

1 tablespoon coriander seeds

1 teaspoon celery salt

1 teaspoon fennel seeds

1 star anise

2 bay leaves

1 sprig fresh, or ½ teaspoon dried,
  thyme

50g/2oz fresh herbs (parsley,
  coriander, a few tarragon sprigs
  and a few basil leaves)

275ml/½ pint dry white wine

Place all the ingredients except the 50g/2oz fresh herbs and the wine in a pan and cover with cold water. Bring to the boil and simmer for 15 minutes, adding the remaining herbs and wine for the last 2 minutes. Cool, cover and refrigerate for at least 36 hours to allow the flavours to develop. Pour the stock through a fine mesh sieve, pressing lightly to extract all the liquid. Either refrigerate and use within 3 days, or freeze. **HM**

CLEAR CHICKEN BROTH

There are a great many ways to use this soup as well as the left-over chicken flesh and vegetables – see overleaf. It is also the basis of Germiny Soup (page 35).

SERVES 12

1 chicken weighing about 1.8kg/4lb, cut in half

3 fresh chicken carcasses, with skin and the 'parson's noses' (which hide a gland with a bitter taste) removed

1 large onion, top and tail removed, skin left on, cut into 3 slices horizontally

350g/12oz onions, cut in half

350g/12oz carrots, left whole

250g/9oz celery

350g/12oz leeks, split in half lengthways, and washed

4 garlic cloves

1 bay leaf

4 sprigs fresh, or 2 teaspoons dried, thyme

150g/5oz white mushrooms

50g/2oz parsley

3 cloves

200g/7oz tinned chopped tomatoes in tomato juice

10g/½oz flaked sea salt

12 lightly crushed black peppercorns

5 sprigs, plus 1 tablespoon chopped, fresh tarragon

Put the chicken halves and carcasses in a large pan. Cover with cold water (about 8.4l/14 pints) and bring to the boil. Skim off any impurities and fat. Meanwhile, heat a frying pan without any fat, add the onion slices with their skin and allow to burn on both sides until completely black (this process will give the chicken soup an amber colour without a burnt flavour). Tip the burnt onion into the pan, and add all the other ingredients except the tablespoon of chopped tarragon. Simmer very gently for 1½–2 hours – the gentleness of the simmering is the key to the clarity of the soup.

Remove the chicken halves, carcasses, vegetables and herbs from the stock and reserve (see below). Line a fine conical sieve with damp muslin, and put the chopped tarragon inside it. Ladle the soup into the sieve and let it filter through slowly without any pressure. Then let the soup settle to allow the fat to rise to the surface (this will take about an hour), and skim off as much of the fat as you can. If you have time, cool and refrigerate the soup so that the fat sets; you will then be able to skim off all the fat more efficiently. Bring to the boil again and reduce to about 3l/5 pints to concentrate the chicken flavour, and add salt only if necessary. **HM**

USES FOR THE LEFT-OVERS

To make chicken noodle soup, add some finely diced chicken, diced cooked mushrooms and, just before serving, some short fine spaghetti (vermicelli) cooked in salted boiling water until it is 'al dente'.

To make a cream soup, blend the cooked vegetables and chicken flesh with some of the chicken soup, and add cream and herbs. Sieve this to make an even smoother soup.

To make a tarragon cream sauce, reduce some of the chicken soup to a syrup and add cream, a squeeze of lemon juice, seasoning and a handful of chopped tarragon. Pour this over the reheated vegetables and sliced chicken flesh and serve with boiled rice as a supper dish.

To make a filling for afternoon-tea sandwiches, slice the chicken flesh and mix with mayonnaise, adding a little curry paste to taste.

VICHYSSOISE OF CUCUMBER

This is usually served ice-cold in the summer, but it is also excellent hot.

SERVES 6-8

50g/2oz butter
350g/12oz leeks, sliced and washed
2 medium onions, thinly sliced
2 garlic cloves, crushed
1 large cucumber, peeled, cut in
   half lengthways and sliced
350g/12oz potatoes, chopped into
   2cm/¾in pieces
2 sprigs fresh, or 1 teaspoon dried,
   thyme
⅓ nutmeg, grated
1.7l/3 pints white chicken stock
   (see page 27)

flaked sea salt
freshly ground black pepper

TO SERVE
½ cucumber, peeled, cut in half
   lengthways, deseeded and finely
   diced
1 tablespoon salt
425ml/¾ pint double cream
2 tablespoons finely chopped
   chives
1 tablespoon finely chopped mint

Melt the butter in a large pan over a medium heat. Add the leeks, onions, garlic and cucumber, together with salt and pepper and a few tablespoons of water. Cook slowly to avoid colouring until transparent. This will take about 10–15 minutes. Add the potatoes, thyme and nutmeg and cover with the chicken stock. Bring to the boil, reduce the heat and simmer for about 30 minutes. Once the potatoes are well cooked, liquidise the soup, then strain it through a fine mesh sieve, pressing down to extract as much of the juices as possible. Check the seasoning, cool and refrigerate.

Meanwhile, sprinkle the diced cucumber with the tablespon of salt and leave for about 30 minutes so that the moisture is drawn out, then rinse in cold water, drain and pat dry (this process makes the cucumber crisper and easier to digest). Tip the diced cucumber into the soup and add the cream, chives and mint. Check the seasoning again, as the colder the soup, the more seasoning it requires. Stir well and serve. **HM**

CHILLED CLEAR TOMATO SOUP

This needs to be started at least one day before you serve it. You can add finely diced vegetables, such as cucumber, tomatoes or celery, or cooked shellfish, such as mussels, prawns or shredded crabmeat, to the soup to make it a more substantial dish for supper.

SERVES 8 GENEROUSLY

5.4kg/12lb vine-ripened tomatoes, cut into 1cm/½in dice

200g/7oz celery sticks, cut into 1cm/½in dice

250g/9oz fennel, cut into 1cm/½in dice

150g/5oz shallots, finely chopped

5–6 garlic cloves, chopped

25g/1oz parsley, chopped but with stalks left on

10g/½oz fresh thyme, chopped but with stalks left on

10g/½oz fresh tarragon, chopped but with stalks left on

50g/2oz fresh basil leaves, chopped but with stalks left on

60g/2½oz flaked sea salt

1 teaspoon celery salt

110g/4oz caster sugar

1 tablespoon Worcestershire sauce

1 teaspoon Tabasco sauce

a pinch of cayenne pepper

Mix the vegetables and herbs in a non-metallic container and sprinkle with the salts, sugar, Worcestershire sauce, Tabasco and cayenne pepper. Stir, cover and marinate for at least 2 or 3 hours, but preferably overnight. Liquidise all the ingredients, then transfer the mixture to a muslin or jelly bag and hang in a cool place for 24 hours to let the juices drip through. Do not squeeze the bag or the soup will be cloudy. Season to taste and chill. **HM**

GERMINY SOUP

This soup does not reheat well, but if you have any left over, it can be liquidised to create a chilled soup of velvet texture and lightness. We use the left-over egg whites to make meringues.

SERVES 6

a25g/1oz butter

200g/7oz sorrel leaves, washed (left
   whole if young, and with stalks
   removed and cut into strips if older)

1l/1¾ pints clear chicken broth
  (see page 31)

10 egg yolks

275ml/½ pint double cream

flaked sea salt

freshly ground black pepper

1 small bunch of chervil,
  finely chopped

Melt the butter in a pan over a medium heat, add the sorrel and stew for a few minutes until it has wilted. Set aside to cool.

Bring the chicken broth to the boil. Whisk the egg yolks and cream together and then pour on half the hot broth, whisking well. Then whisk this into the remaining broth. Cook gently, stirring continuously with a wooden spoon, but do not let it boil. As soon as the soup is thick enough to coat the back of a wooden spoon, add the cold sorrel and take off the heat. Apart from flavouring the soup, the sorrel will stop the temperature of the soup rising and prevent it from curdling. Season to taste and serve sprinkled with the chopped chervil. **HM**

RED ONION AND SMOKED BACON SOUP WITH RAREBIT SOLDIERS

SERVES 6

110g/4oz butter

6 red onions, finely sliced

2 garlic cloves, chopped

1 tablespoon plain flour

425ml/¾ pint dry white wine

1.5l/2½ pints brown chicken stock
   (see page 28)

1 bay leaf, 1 sprig of fresh thyme and
   12 peppercorns, wrapped in a piece
   of muslin and secured with string

200g/7oz streaky smoked bacon, in
   one piece with no rind

flaked sea salt

freshly ground black pepper

FOR THE RAREBIT SOLDIERS

20g/¾oz butter

10g/½oz plain flour

55ml/2fl oz milk, warmed

250g/9oz mature cheddar cheese,
   grated

1 tablespoon Dijon mustard

55ml/2fl oz stout

1 tablespoon Worcestershire sauce

freshly ground black pepper

1 egg

3 slices of bread

Start by making the soup. Melt the butter in a heavy-bottomed pan over a medium heat. Add the onions and garlic and cook slowly for about 15–20 minutes, stirring occasionally, until they caramelise. Stir in the flour, and then the wine. Bring to the boil and simmer for a few minutes to reduce the acidity of the wine. Add the brown chicken stock, the bag of herbs and the smoked bacon piece. Bring to the boil again and simmer for a further 30 minutes and then strain the soup. Discard the muslin bag, set aside the bacon and one-third of the onions. Liquidise the remaining two-thirds of the strained onions and return to the soup. Now pass the soup through a fine mesh sieve, pressing all the juices through with the back of a spoon. Dice the bacon into 5mm/¼in pieces and tip these into the soup with the reserved cooked onions. Reheat the soup before serving, check the seasoning, and hand the rarebit soldiers separately.

To make the rarebit soldiers, melt the butter in a small pan over a low heat and stir in the flour. Cook for a few minutes, but do not let it colour. Whisk in the milk and continue to whisk until the sauce comes to the boil and thickens. Remove from the heat and add the cheese, mustard, stout, Worcestershire sauce and pepper. Return to a low heat and stir until well combined. Take off the heat, whisk in the egg and cool.

Turn the grill to high. Lightly toast the bread on both sides. Spread the cheese mixture on the toast and grill until nicely brown. Cut each slice of toast into four fingers, or 'soldiers'. **HM**

CURRIED JERUSALEM ARTICHOKE SOUP

SERVES 6-8

200g/7oz butter

2 medium onions, diced

4 garlic cloves, crushed

2 celery sticks, finely sliced

4 tablespoons curry powder

900g/2lb Jerusalem artichokes, diced and kept in acidulated water (juice of 1 lemon per 1l/1¾ pints water) to avoid discolouration

250g/9oz potatoes, diced

1 sprig fresh, or ½ teaspoon dried, thyme

1 x 400g/14oz tin of chopped tomatoes in tomato juice

75g/3oz fresh coriander leaves

2.25l/4 pints white chicken stock or vegetable stock (see page 27 or 30)

570ml/1 pint double cream

flaked sea salt

freshly ground black pepper

50g/2oz toasted flaked almonds

Melt the butter in a heavy-bottomed pan over a medium heat. Add the onions, garlic and celery and cook for a few minutes until they become transparent. Mix in the curry powder and stir-fry for a few more minutes to release the full flavour of the spices.

Drain the artichokes and add them to the pan together with the potatoes, thyme, tomatoes and juice, and half the coriander. Cover with the stock, stir, and season lightly. Bring to the boil, skim off any impurities and simmer for about 20 minutes until the vegetables are soft. Strain.

Liquidise the vegetables with some of the stock and strain these through a fine mesh sieve, pressing with the back of a spoon to extract all the juices. Add the remaining stock until the consistency is to your liking.

Shortly before serving, add the cream, bring to the boil, check the seasoning and garnish with the remaining coriander leaves and the flaked almonds. HM

LEEK AND STILTON SOUP

This can be made up to 3 days in advance, and then reheated very slowly.

	NUMBER OF SERVINGS	
	8	40
butter	50g/2oz	250g/10oz
onions, finely chopped	100g/4oz	500g/1lb 4oz
leeks, sliced in half lengthwise,		
washed and shredded finely	300g/12oz	1.6kg/3lb 8oz
potatoes, cut into 1cm/½in dice	250g/10oz	1.2kg/3lb
vegetable stock (see page 30)	1l/2 pints	5l/10 pints
Stilton cheese, with rind removed	200g/8oz	1.2kg/2lb 8oz
whipping cream	125ml/¼ pint	625ml/1¼ pints
freshly ground black pepper		

Melt the butter in a heavy-bottomed pan, add the onions and cook gently for about 10 minutes so that they soften but do not colour. Add the leeks and cook until they are soft. Add the potatoes and cook for 1–2 minutes, without allowing them to colour. Add the stock, bring to the boil and simmer for 20 minutes or until the potatoes are 'falling'.

Blend the soup until smooth, then crumble in the Stilton and stir over a low heat until it melts. Make sure there are no lumps, but do not allow it to boil. Remove from the heat. Check the seasoning and swirl in the cream. PG

BRUNCH

Having seen beautiful breakfasts made for young guests – first of my son and now of my grandson – remain untouched because they were still sound asleep till late morning, we gave up and started having Sunday brunch at midday. It has been a huge success, partly because all are ready for it by then and partly because of the food.

There are usually some years in childhood when nearly every dish is refused and mothers are worried as well as irritated at having taken a lot of trouble only to see their efforts wasted. When one of my nephews was about eight he said no to everything and was painfully thin. My sister coaxed him with 'Oh, come on, darling. It's delicious.' 'I *hate* delicious food,' he answered. Then they suddenly get hungry. I love watching young men of cricket-playing age eat all that is put before them and come back for more, instead of pushing it about on their plate.

Everyone's favourites are here and they seem to go well together, a spoonful of each, and the piled plate is soon clean again. Coffee, tea, orange juice and water are on the side. The feast is finished off with pancakes and maple syrup. You can dawdle, read the awful Sunday papers, take second or third helpings and, when at last you are full, it is still early afternoon. **DD**

CHATSWORTH MUESLI

This is served in the bar of the Bath and Racquets Club, in London, which is owned and run by that perfectionist Mark Birley, who knows exactly how to please his customers. **DD**

MAKES 1KG/2¼LB

110g/4oz clear honey
75g/3oz sesame seeds
40g/1½oz pine kernels
50g/2oz desiccated coconut
75g/3oz sunflower seeds
75g/3oz wheat flakes
85g/3½oz hazelnuts

110g/4oz porridge oats
50g/2oz banana chips
75g/3oz breakfast bran
110g/4oz sultanas
75g/3oz coarse bran
35g/1½oz pumpkin seeds
70ml/2½fl oz sunflower oil

Preheat the oven to 220C/425F/Gas 7. Put the honey in a bowl and warm it in a pan of nearly boiling water to make the honey runny enough to mix easily with the other ingredients.

Toast the sesame seeds and pine kernels (separately) in the oven for 5–10 minutes, turning occasionally, until golden brown. Add these to all the other dried ingredients and mix well. Add the warmed honey and the oil and mix thoroughly.

The muesli will keep for 6 weeks in an airtight container stored in a cool dry place. **AB**

SMOKED HADDOCK KEDGEREE
WITH CURRY SAUCE

The curry sauce underlines kedgeree's Indian origins and is a big improvement on the usual bland mixture found in this country. **DD**

SERVES 6

600g/1lb 6oz undyed Finnan haddock
    fillets, skinned and any bones
    removed
425ml/¾ pint milk
150ml/¼ pint double cream
6 free range eggs, hard-boiled, peeled,
    and cut in half lengthways
flaked sea salt
freshly ground black pepper

FOR THE CURRY SAUCE
50g/2oz clarified butter
200g/7oz onions, finely chopped
2 garlic cloves, finely chopped
1 bay leaf
1 sprig fresh, or 1 teaspoon dried,
    thyme

2 heaped teaspoons Madras curry
    powder
350g/12oz tomatoes, skinned and
    cut into quarters
150g/5oz eating apples, peeled,
    cored and coarsely diced
25g/1oz raisins
150ml/¼ pint milk
2 tablespoons coarsely chopped
    fresh coriander leaves

FOR THE BAKED RICE
50g/2oz clarified butter
250g/9oz onions, finely chopped
1 garlic clove, finely chopped
300g/11oz long grain rice
1 tablespoon chopped parsley

Preheat the oven to 180C/350F/Gas 4.

Cut the haddock fillets in half along their length, place in a saucepan and add the milk and cream (they should just cover the fish). Bring to a simmer, cover, turn off the heat and leave to stand for 5–10 minutes. Strain the liquid and reserve. Flake the fish.

Meanwhile make the curry sauce. Melt the butter in a pan, add the onions, garlic, bay leaf and thyme, and cook over a medium heat until they are browned, stirring frequently. Stir in the curry powder, tomatoes, apples and raisins, and cook for a further few minutes. Add about 200ml/7fl oz boiling water and cook for about 20 minutes until the mixture thickens to a chunky purée. Add the milk and cook until the mixture is creamy. Season to taste, add the coriander and keep warm.

To cook the baked rice, melt the butter in a small ovenproof pan, add the onions and garlic and cook over a moderate heat, stirring constantly so that the onions soften but do not colour. (Adding a little salt and a tablespoon or two of water after a few minutes may help this process.) Stir in the rice and cook for a couple of minutes. Pour in the poaching liquid from the fish, turn up the heat and bring to the boil, stirring to prevent the rice sticking. Take off the heat, cover tightly and bake in the oven for 15 minutes.

Turn down the oven to 150C/300F/Gas 2. Take the rice out and, while it is still hot, gently fold in the flaked fish and the eggs and transfer to a serving dish. Cover with foil and return to the oven for a few minutes to allow the eggs and fish to warm up with the rice.

To serve, sprinkle with the chopped parsley, and hand the curry sauce separately. **HM**

DEVILLED LAMBS' KIDNEYS

Start preparing the kidneys the day before you want to serve them.

SERVES 6

12 lambs' kidneys, fat and skin
   removed
75g/3oz clarified butter
60g/2½oz shallots, finely chopped
100ml/4fl oz dry white wine
150ml/¼ pint double cream
150ml/¼ pint brown chicken stock
   (see page 28)
1 tablespoon anchovy purée
2 tablespoons chopped parsley

FOR THE MARINADE
3 tablespoons mushroom ketchup
3 tablespoons Worcestershire sauce
3 tablespoons ready-made English
   mustard
1 garlic clove, finely chopped
1 sprig fresh, or ½ teaspoon dried,
   thyme
1 bay leaf

Holding a kidney flat under one hand on a chopping board, slice it into two halves horizontally with the other hand, and then remove the core (sinew) of the kidney, using a small sharp pointed knife. Repeat for the other kidneys.

Make the marinade by combining all the ingredients. Pour it over the kidneys, mix well, cover and refrigerate overnight.

When you are ready to cook, remove the kidneys from the marinade and reserve the liquid. Heat the butter in a large sauté pan. Fry the kidneys for about 2 minutes on each side until they are firm, then transfer them to a warm plate to rest. Add the shallots to the pan and cook for 1 minute. Pour in the wine and the reserved kidney marinade and bring them to the boil. Add the cream, stock and anchovy purée and simmer until the mixture is reduced to a coating consistency. Strain this through a fine sieve into another pan. Add the rested kidneys and any juices and reheat for a minute or two before tipping on to a warm serving dish. Serve sprinkled with the chopped parsley. **HM**

CORNED BEEF HASH

We use a deep fryer to cook the potatoes, but it is possible to sauté parboiled potatoes in vegetable oil for a similar effect.

SERVES 6

675g/1lb 8oz potatoes (preferably
  Marfona, Maris Piper or Concorde)
50g/2oz butter
1 medium onion, finely chopped
1 clove garlic, finely chopped
675g/1lb 8oz corned beef (about 2 tins),
  cut into 2cm/¾in dice

a dash of Worcestershire sauce
oil for deep frying, or 150ml/¼ pint
  vegetable oil for sautéing
flaked sea salt
freshly ground black pepper

If you are using a deep fryer, turn it to 150C/300F. Peel and dice the potatoes to make 2cm/¾in cubes. Wash these to get rid of some of the excess starch and dry thoroughly in a tea towel. Either blanch (part cook) in the fryer for 5–7 minutes, or parboil the potatoes for 3–5 minutes and then drain.

Meanwhile, melt the butter in a frying pan and cook the onion and garlic over a low heat until they are transparent. Add the corned beef and cook until it just starts to break down. Add the Worcestershire sauce, take off the heat and set aside.

Preheat the oven to 200C/400F/Gas 6, and either turn the fryer up to 180C/350F or set the vegetable oil to heat in a large sauté pan. Deep fry, or sauté, the potatoes until golden brown and then mix into the corned beef mixture. Season to taste. Pile into a greased ovenproof dish and bake for 35–40 minutes. **DW**

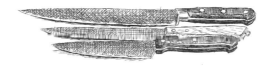

PORK SPARE RIBS

The ribs should be marinated for at least 10–12 hours, so start the day before you want to eat them. Any left-over cooked sauce will freeze well and makes an excellent, spicy accompaniment to grilled meat, poultry or even fish.

SERVES 6

6 racks of pork ribs, each weighing
    about 550g/1lb 4oz (6–8 single ribs
    per rack)
1 tablespoon chopped parsley

FOR THE MARINADE
350g/12oz onions, finely chopped
4 garlic cloves, finely chopped
1 tablespoon dried sage
a pinch of dried thyme
2 bay leaves
½ teaspoon chilli flakes

½ teaspoon coarsely ground black
    pepper
juice of 2 lemons
1 teaspoon Tabasco sauce
175g/6oz light muscavado sugar
110ml/4fl oz dark soy sauce
110ml/4fl oz light soy sauce
110g/4oz tomato purée
1 tablespoon clear honey
200ml/7fl oz tomato ketchup
570ml/1 pint Worcestershire sauce

Mix together all the marinade ingredients in a non-metallic bowl. Cut the pork into single spare ribs, add to the marinade, mixing well, and then seal the bowl with clingfilm and refrigerate overnight.

When you are ready to cook, preheat the oven to 180C/350F/Gas 4. Spread the ribs out on a deep roasting tray or ovenproof dish, and pour over the marinade. Seal with foil and bake for about 1¼ hours, by which time the meat will be tender but not falling off the bone, and the marinade will have turned into a dark sauce.

Serve sprinkled with the chopped parsley. HM

ROSTI POTATOES

This grated potato cake can be made in advance and reheated in the oven. You can vary the ingredients, using equal quantities of potato and either celeriac, parsnip or carrot. Rosti also makes a good accompaniment for grilled meat, poultry or fish.

SERVES 6

670g/1lb 8oz potatoes   flaked sea salt
110g/4oz clarified butter   freshly ground black pepper

Preheat the oven to 180C/350F/Gas 4. Before you start, it is worth remembering that once you have grated the potatoes, they should be cooked as soon as possible to prevent them releasing too much moisture.

Peel enough potatoes to make 500g/1lb 2oz when grated. Grate them coarsely and season them.

Heat the butter in a heavy, ovenproof frying pan (about 20cm/8in in diameter) and add the potatoes. Using a fish slice, press down to level the potatoes and help the mixture stick together. Fry on a moderate heat for a few minutes. Make sure the potatoes do not stick to the pan – if they start to do so, loosen around the edges and reach underneath with the fish slice. Once the underneath of the potatoes is golden in colour, pour what remains of the melted butter into a container by tilting the pan and holding the potatoes firmly with the fish slice to stop them sliding. Turn the potato cake over, then pour the butter back into the pan and fry for another 2–3 minutes. Check the rosti is not sticking to the pan, then transfer it to the oven for about 10 minutes until it is crisp and cooked through.

To serve, drain off any excess butter, and slice into 6 wedges. **DW**

PANCAKES

These pancakes are slightly thicker than usual because the self-raising flour gives them a slight lift, and the golden syrup gives them a slightly sweet smell. They are usually served with maple syrup and Devonshire Cream (see page 150).

MAKES 20 PANCAKES

450g/1lb self-raising flour

½ teaspoon salt

75g/3oz caster sugar

4 eggs

570ml/1 pint milk

6 tablespoons golden syrup, warmed

2 tablespoons clarified butter

Sieve the flour, salt and sugar into a large bowl. In another bowl, whisk the eggs into the milk, and mix in the warmed syrup. Put the butter into a heatproof container.

Make a well in the centre of the flour and start to pour in the liquid, whisking constantly until the batter is the consistency of thick, pouring cream. Leave to rest for 10 minutes.

Melt a tablespoon of the butter in a frying, or crêpe, pan. Swirl it round and pour off the excess into the remaining butter. When the pan is hot, ladle in about half a cup/4 tablespoons of batter. Turn down the heat a little. Tip the pan so that the batter spreads evenly over the base. Cook for 45 seconds–1 minute until the pancake is golden brown underneath, and then flip it over. Cook until the other side is golden brown, then slide it on to a warm plate and cover with a clean damp tea towel.

Repeat until all the pancake mixture is used up. **DW**

EGGS

A S A POULTRY KEEPER of seventy-five years' standing, I am particularly interested in egg receipts. The diet of the hens is naturally all-important, and daily access to fresh grass has an effect on the colour of the yolk. I am a strong believer in whole wheat and maize as part of their food, so mine have those as well as Layers Pellets.

The game larder in the park was built in 1910 to hang 4,000 pheasants. It is a listed building, in the style of Wyatville, stone, with a grand mosaic floor – the sort of structure the planners would not allow in a Grade I park now. It was doing nothing, so we made perches and nesting boxes and in go pullets on 'point of lay' bought from a mass producer of poultry. To accustom them to their new home and ensure that they return there to roost, they are shut in for three or four days when they first arrive. After the pop holes are opened, the boldest has a look at the wider world and the acres of parkland at her disposal. One by one they all step out and find undreamed-of luxuries – worms galore, fresh grass, earth for dust baths, grit from the roadside and all else that goes with real 'free range' and is the delight of the hen-who-has-everything.

When I think of their flock sisters confined in battery cages, our hens should thank their lucky stars that they have landed in a poultry paradise. All these blessings are transferred to their eggs, which go daily to our kitchen and the Farm Shop. Quality is the thing – proper shells and orange yolks. People come from miles away to find them in the shop, where they are in a corner of their own, piled in a straw-lined basket. They are all colours known to eggs (except green – I haven't got Aracaunas; I think blue-green eggs look as if they are beginning to go bad). Dark brown come from the Welsummers, lighter brown from the Rhode Island Reds, white from White Leghorns and ordinary egg colour from the 'commercial' cross-breeds. The customers can choose their favourites, but they sometimes break a few when digging in the basket for their preferred colour.

A love of poultry seems to run in my family. When Nancy lived in the rue Monsieur in Paris, she had the best *bonne à tout faire* ever in the

person of Marie. A true peasant from the middle of France, Marie
was an excellent cook. Once she bought a live hen at the market for
some future lunch party. The next day there was an egg in the basket.
The hen was reprieved and lived for a long time, roosting in the oven
and laying daily. Her existence confirmed the view of some of Nancy's
acquaintances that they had a mad Englishwoman among them.

Now Delia has taught us how to boil an egg, explaining the method
in detail (Nancy did not live to profit by her advice), and half the
population own her books. But there is no mention of where the egg
came from, although she does explain how to tell its age by immersing
it in boiling water. To get a decent egg it seems to me that you must
keep your own hens. **DD**

POACHED EGGS MEURETTE

We serve this as a first course with brown bread and butter, or for supper with the eggs on a bed of Caramelised Chicory (see page 144).

SERVES 8 AS A FIRST COURSE, OR 4 AS A MAIN COURSE

8 very fresh eggs

2 tablespoons chopped parsley

FOR THE MEURETTE SAUCE

570 ml/1 pint red wine

8 button onions or shallots, each
　weighing about 25g/1oz, cut in half

4 garlic cloves

2 level teaspoons caster sugar

1 bay leaf

1 sprig fresh, or ½ teaspoon dried,
　thyme

2 sprigs fresh tarragon

160g/6oz rindless smoked streaky
　bacon rashers

150g/5oz white button mushrooms

150ml/¼ pint reduced brown chicken
　stock (see page 28)

25g/1oz butter

FOR THE POACHING LIQUID

1.2l/2 pints water

150ml/¼ pint red wine

55ml/2fl oz red wine vinegar

Make the sauce by bringing the wine to the boil and adding the button onion or shallot halves, garlic cloves, caster sugar, bay leaf, thyme and tarragon. Simmer for 10 minutes. Lift out the onions and garlic and set these aside.

Cut the bacon into 5mm/¼in strips and fry over a high heat for a few minutes until the bacon fat starts to run. Add the button mushrooms and the reserved onions or shallots and garlic cloves. Lower the heat to moderate and cook until the ingredients are soft. Drain off the fat and set aside.

Meanwhile, reduce the red wine liquor to a syrupy consistency. Add the stock and again reduce until there is about 100ml/4fl oz left. Pass this sauce through a fine mesh sieve, then reheat it, adding the butter and the bacon mixture, and keep warm.

Combine the poaching liquid ingredients in a wide pan and bring to a simmer. Crack the eggs into this and poach for about 2½ minutes. (It is easiest to cook 2 or 3 eggs at a time.) When they are set but still soft, lift the eggs out on to a clean tea towel to drain.

To serve, place the eggs on a warmed dish, spoon over the sauce and sprinkle with the chopped parsley. **HM**

POACHED EGGS WITH FRIED CAPERS AND PARSLEY BUTTER

This is a popular and easy-to-make first course, although it does require last-minute cooking. We serve it with brown bread and butter.

SERVES 6

6 heaped tablespoons pickled capers in vinegar	**55ml/2fl oz white wine vinegar**
	6 eggs
6 tablespoons clarified butter	**3 tablespoons chopped parsley**

Squeeze out the excess vinegar from the capers and dry on a paper towel. Melt the butter over a high heat until it is smoking and fry the capers, stirring continuously, until they are brown and crunchy. This should take about 5–7 minutes. Take off the heat, lift the capers out with a slotted spoon, and set aside. Set the frying pan with the butter to one side.

Bring about 570ml/1 pint of water to the boil, add the vinegar and reduce the heat so that the water is just simmering. Crack the eggs straight into the water (it is easiest to cook 3 at a time) and poach for 3–4 minutes. Drain the eggs on a clean tea towel and then place one on each of 6 small warm plates.

Reheat the butter, add the capers for a minute, then add the parsley. It will snap and crackle for a few seconds; as soon as it stops, take it off the heat. Put a tablespoon of capers and parsley on each egg and pour over a little butter. Serve immediately. **HM**

EGG MOUSSE

Writing the menus for our Carriage House Restaurant, I tried to use English words, but somehow they were not tempting. Baker's Wife's Potatoes is an impossible name for the delicious pommes de terre boulangère. *If you turn Burnt Cream, Paste, Green Beans, Cheese Tart and Clear Soup into Crème Brulée, Pâté, Haricots Verts, Quiche and Consommé, they immediately sound better. Soufflé, mayonnaise and omelette have crept into our dictionary, and there is no English word for mousse. If it was anglicised as 'mouse' it somehow wouldn't do. You will remember in* The Tale of the Pie and the Patty Pan *by Beatrix Potter, how when Duchess, the little black dog, accepts an invitation to tea with Ribby the cat, and Ribby tells her she is baking a pie of something delicious, Duchess gets very agitated and says to herself she hopes it isn't mouse. Most people would agree with her.* DD

SERVES 8

7 hard-boiled eggs	a few drops of Tabasco sauce
2 leaves of gelatine	2 tablespoons chopped parsley
2 tablespoons dry vermouth	1 tablespoon chopped chervil
200ml/7fl oz chicken stock (see	1 tablespoon chopped chives
page 27)	1 tablespoon chopped corriander leaves
425ml/¾ pint mayonnaise	200ml/7fl oz double cream, whipped
2 tablespoons medium curry paste	flaked sea salt
a pinch of mace	freshly ground black pepper
a dash of Worcestershire sauce	

Shell the hard-boiled eggs, cut them in half and separate the whites from the yolks. Dice the whites and mash the yolks.

Break up the gelatine leaves, pour the vermouth over them and leave to rehydrate for 5 minutes, before dissolving them in a pan over a low heat.

Combine the stock and mayonnaise, and whisk in the curry paste, mace and the Worcestershire and Tabasco sauces. Stir in the chopped egg whites, the egg yoks and warm gelatine mixture. Cool the mixture rapidly by placing the bowl in a basin filled with ice cubes and water. As the mixture begins to set, stir it now and then until it is all the consistency of a thick sauce. Then add the herbs and fold in the cream. Check the seasoning and pour into a 1.2l/2 pint soufflé dish and refrigerate for 2–3 hours until set. **DW**

OEUFS À LA TRIPE

This is another example of the sort of muddle you can get into with the naming of dishes. Tripe has no part in this one; it is just an excellent concoction of sliced hard-boiled eggs and onions in béchamel sauce, a first course that was a favourite of my mother's. **DD**

SERVES 12 AS A FIRST COURSE, OR 6 AS A LUNCH DISH

18 free range eggs	1.35l/2¼ pints milk
1 tablespoon salt	flaked sea salt
175g/6oz butter	freshly ground black pepper
700g/1½lb onions, finely sliced	½ nutmeg, grated
75g/3oz plain flour	

Cook the eggs by placing them in a pan, sprinkling them with the 1 tablespoon of salt and pouring in enough boiling water to cover them. Bring back to the boil and simmer for 8 minutes. Remove from the heat, run cold water over the eggs until they are cool enough to handle, then shell and set aside.

To make the sauce, melt the butter over a low heat and add the onions. Sprinkle with a pinch of salt and cook until they are soft but not coloured. Add the flour and stir for a minute or two, again without letting them colour. In another pan, bring the milk to the boil and gradually pour this over the onion mixture, stirring to make a creamy sauce. Season with salt, pepper and grated nutmeg. Simmer for 10 minutes, stirring occasionally to prevent the sauce from sticking.

To serve, slice the eggs into 3 and add to the sauce, mixing gently to avoid breaking up the eggs. **HM**

EGG CROQUETTES
WITH PORTUGAISE SAUCE

The Portugaise tomato sauce can be made a day or two in advance. The final stage of the cooking the croquettes requires a deep fryer.

SERVES 6

9 eggs

1 tablespoon salt

200g/7oz flour

75g/3oz parsley sprigs to garnish

flaked sea salt

freshly ground black pepper

FOR THE PORTUGAISE SAUCE

25g/1oz butter

2 tablespoons olive oil

2 shallots, finely chopped

3 garlic cloves, finely chopped

1 tablespoon tomato purée

1 sprig fresh, or 1 teaspoon dried, thyme

1 bay leaf

900g/2lb tomatoes, skinned, deseeded and diced

FOR THE BÉCHAMEL SAUCE

150ml/¼ pint milk

150ml/¼ pint cream

1 bay leaf

½ clove

⅓ nutmeg, grated

1 button onion, finely shredded

25g/1oz butter

25g/1oz flour

3 egg yolks

2 tablespoons Worcestershire sauce

a dash of Tabasco sauce

2 tablespoons chopped chives

FOR THE CRUMBING

3 eggs, beaten well

100ml/4fl oz oil

200g/7oz fresh white breadcrumbs

Start by making the Portugaise sauce. Melt the butter with the olive oil in a frying pan. Add the shallots and cook over a medium heat until they are soft but not coloured. Add the garlic, tomato purée, thyme and bay leaf, and cook for a minute longer before adding two-thirds of the diced tomatoes. Season lightly and simmer for 30 minutes. Take off the heat, discard the thyme and bay leaf, and then blend the mixture in a food processor. Return the purée to the pan, add the remaining diced tomatoes and cook for a further few minutes until the sauce thickens slightly. Check the seasoning, cover and put aside. (Cool and refrigerate the sauce at this stage if you want to reheat it later.)

Cook the 9 eggs by placing them in a pan, sprinkling them with the tablespoon of salt and pouring in enough boiling water to cover them. Bring back to the boil and simmer for 8 minutes. Remove from the heat, run cold water over the eggs until they are cool enough to handle, then shell, chop coarsely and keep on one side.

To make the béchamel sauce, start by bringing the milk and cream to the boil with the bay leaf, clove, nutmeg and onion. Then set this aside to infuse for 10 minutes.

Meanwhile melt the butter over a low heat in a pan big enough to hold the milk and cream. Add the flour and stir for a minute or two without letting it brown. Take the pan off the heat and strain in the milk and cream, whisking to make a smooth sauce. Simmer gently for about 5 minutes, stirring frequently. Remove from the heat and stir in the 3 egg yolks, Worcestershire sauce, Tabasco sauce and chives. Return to a low heat and cook until the mixture thickens. Add the chopped eggs, check the seasoning, and then spread mixture on a lightly buttered tray. To prevent a skin forming on its surface, cover with clingfilm and allow to cool.

To form the croquettes, divide the mixture into 12 equal portions and, using the flour to prevent the mixture from sticking to your fingers, shape it into balls. Roll these in the flour.

To crumb the croquettes, whisk together the 3 eggs with the oil, and season well with salt and pepper. Dip the balls into this, and then into the breadcrumbs. Now mould into croquette shapes, place on a tray and refrigerate if you are not using immediately.

Before serving, turn the deep fryer to 180C/350F, and meanwhile reheat the sauce. Deep fry the croquettes for 3–5 minutes until golden brown. Serve immediately garnished with fresh or deep-fried sprigs of parsley, and hand the sauce separately. HM

OMELETTE WITH ONIONS AND CROUTONS

Omelettes are best made in small quantities. This is why the receipt is for 2 people. You can multiply all the ingredients, but don't cook more than 6 eggs at any one time. Omelettes should be eaten as soon as possible, so they remain moist – what the French call 'baveuse'. As with soufflés, guests should wait for their omelettes, not the other way around.

SERVES 2

100g/4oz clarified butter
1 red onion (120g/4½oz), finely
   sliced
40g/1½oz white bread, cut into
   1cm/½in dice

35g/1½oz butter
6 free range eggs
flaked sea salt
freshly ground black pepper
1 tablespoon chopped parsley

Melt 25g/1oz of the clarified butter in a small frying pan, add the onion slices with a pinch of salt and 2 tablespoons of water and cook on a moderate heat for about 15 minutes until they are brown and caramelised. Set aside.

Now melt the remaining clarified butter in an omelette pan on a moderate heat, add the diced bread and cook until crisp and golden, tossing regularly. Drain, and add to the onion.

Butter an oval serving dish with 10g/½oz of the butter and keep warm.

Beat the eggs with salt and pepper, and add the chopped parsley, and the onion slices and croutons.

Heat the remaining 25g/1oz of butter in an omelette pan over a medium heat until it is foaming, but do not let it brown. Pour in the egg mixture, turn the heat higher and cook rapidly, stirring constantly, preferably with a fork, until the eggs are just set but still soft on the top. Take off the heat and, using a spatula, fold opposite sides of the omelette in towards the centre.

Turn out the omelette, seam-side down, on to the warm serving dish and serve at once. **HM**

FIRST COURSES, LIGHT LUNCHES & SUPPERS

I s it because you are hungry that the first food you are offered is often the best? Or is it because of its own excellence?

In a restaurant it is often tempting to ask for two first courses rather than one followed by a main course. First courses are certainly my favourites, and the following receipts seem to go down well whatever the time of day or evening. Of these, my mother's gnocchi is the one I like best. Grilled tomatoes look and taste good with them, and the two together are a meal in themselves. The addition of a sympathetic vegetable would make most of the receipts into a good supper.

The Hartington Quiche is named after the Stilton cheese that is made at Hartington. This Peak District village has all the essentials of a green and a duck pond, and lots of pubs built higgledy-piggledy before planning was invented – an entirely pleasing scene, made all the better by its cheese. (Only cheese made in Nottinghamshire, Leicestershire and Derbyshire can be officially called Stilton.) It is no wonder this quiche is popular in the Carriage House Restaurant.

Marquess of Hartington is a 'courtesy title' of the Duke of Devonshire. The best-known bearer of the name, till he inherited the dukedom aged twenty-one, was the 6th Duke, the 'Bachelor' Duke, called Hart by his intimates. Having no wife, he interested himself in all domestic details and food was at the top of the list. It was he who built the vast kitchen in his north wing of Chatsworth. He described it in his *Handbook* of 1844 thus: '*The kitchen itself is handsome and spacious, and contains steam-cupboards, and a hot steam-table; and wood is the sole fuel employed in the huge grate, as well as coke for the steam contrivances, which, diminishing the quantity of blacks, must greatly add to the cleanliness of the place. There is a good arrangement for preserving fish alive in water, till the moment of execution. The pastry convenient, the scullery awful, and the larder atrocious; for, although it may be airy and highly convenient for salting, it looks into the abysses of a dusty coal-yard.*' The openings for the vast stoves are still there. The kitchen and its neighbouring rooms are now the carpenters' shop, a repository for out-of-season garden notices and a mess room. **DD**

MY MOTHER'S GNOCCHI

For supper, we usually accompany this with Slow-Baked Tomatoes (page 143) and Spinach with Sorrel (page 140).

SERVES 12 AS A FIRST COURSE, OR 6 AS A SUPPER DISH

175g/6oz butter
425ml/¾ pint water
175g/6oz strong flour
6 eggs
175g/6oz grated Parmesan
3 tablespoons double cream
½ teaspoon grated nutmeg

flaked sea salt
freshly ground black pepper

FOR THE TOPPING
425ml/¾ pint double cream
40g/1½oz butter
125g/4½oz grated Parmesan

Put the butter in a pan, add the water and bring to the boil. As soon as it boils, take the pan off the heat and tip in all the flour at once, mixing it to a smooth paste with a wooden spoon. Return to a gentle heat and cook until the paste leaves the sides of the pan. Either transfer the paste into the bowl of an electric mixer fixed with paddle attachment, and beat on medium speed while the mixture cools down slightly, or divide it into 2 portions in order to beat by hand. Then add one egg at a time, beating well between each. Stir in the cheese and cream and season to taste with nutmeg, salt and pepper.

Preheat the oven to 180C/350F/Gas 4.

Bring a wide pan of water to a gentle simmer. Do not let it boil because it may cause the gnocchi to break up. Using two lightly oiled teaspoons, shape the mixture into oval dumplings the size of quails' eggs. Lower about half of them into the water at a time, and poach for 4–5 minutes. They are cooked when they feel springy to the touch. Lift them out using a draining spoon and put them into very cold water to refresh them. Drain, and arrange in an ovenproof dish, spreading them out to allow them to rise properly. For the topping, cover the gnocchi with the cream, dot with the butter, and sprinkle with Parmesan. Bake for about 20–25 minutes until the gnocchi have nearly doubled in size and a golden-brown skin forms on the surface. HM

TWICE-BAKED PARMESAN AND GOATS' CHEESE SOUFFLÉS

These can be made 1–2 days ahead and reheated. For supper, we usually serve these on a bed of buttered spinach, accompanied by a seasonal salad with celery and walnuts.

SERVES 12

110g/4oz butter
110g/4oz plain flour
300ml/11fl oz milk
½ nutmeg, grated
a few drops of Tabasco sauce or
   a pinch of cayenne pepper
110g/4oz freshly grated Parmesan
110g/4oz semi-mature goats' cheese
5 egg yolks
10 egg whites
a pinch of cream of tartar or a few
   drops of lemon juice
flaked sea salt
freshly ground black pepper

TO LINE THE RAMEKINS
110g/4oz soft butter
110g/4oz fresh white or brown
   breadcrumbs
25g/1oz freshly grated Parmesan

FOR THE CREAM SAUCE
60g/2½oz butter
60g/2½oz plain flour
640ml/23fl oz milk
720ml/1¼ pints double cream
½ nutmeg, grated

FOR THE TOPPING
110g/4oz semi-mature goats' cheese,
   cut into 10g/½oz pieces
110g/4oz freshly grated Parmesan

Preheat the oven to 180C/350F/Gas 4. Grease 12 ramekins, each 7.5cm/3in in diameter and 4cm/1½in deep, generously with the soft butter using a brush. Dust the insides with the breadcrumbs mixed with the Parmesan, shaking off any excess. Divide the ramekins between 2 deep roasting tins and set aside.

To make the soufflés, start by melting the butter in a pan over a moderate heat and whisking in the flour. Cook for a few minutes without browning, whisking regularly. Put this roux on one side to cool. Bring the milk to the boil, and season well with nutmeg, salt and pepper, and the Tabasco sauce or cayenne pepper. Add the cooled roux, whisking continuously until the mixture becomes a smooth but thick sauce. Remove from the heat and, with a wooden spoon, beat in both cheeses and then the egg yolks.

In a clean bowl, whisk the egg whites with a pinch of cream of tartar or a few drops of lemon juice until they form soft peaks. Whisk a third of the egg whites into the cheese mixture to loosen it, and then pour the loosened mixture into the remaining egg whites, folding it in delicately with a large metal spoon. Fill the ramekins nearly to the top with the soufflé mixture.

Pour enough boiling water into the roasting tins to come halfway up the ramekins and simmer for a few minutes on top of the stove, then transfer the tins to the oven and cook for 20–25 minutes until the soufflés are springy to the touch. Take the ramekins out of the roasting tins and rest them in a cool place for 15 minutes. (The soufflés can be cooled, turned out, wrapped individually in clingfilm and frozen at this stage.) Turn them out on to 2 ovenproof dishes (on a bed of buttered spinach if you are serving them this way), leaving a gap between each, because they will double in size when baked again.

To make the cream sauce, melt the butter in a pan over a moderate heat and whisk in the flour. Cook for a few minutes without browning, whisking regularly. Put this roux on one side to cool. Bring the milk and cream to the boil, and season lightly with nutmeg, salt and pepper. Add to the cooled roux, whisking continuously until the mixture becomes a smooth cream sauce, and cook for a further minute.

Pour the sauce over the soufflés, masking each one. Top each with the goats' cheese and Parmesan. (The dishes can be set aside and refrigerated at this stage for 1–2 days.) Bake for 25–30 minutes until doubled in size. Serve at once. **HM**

CHEESE, HAM AND ONION SOUFFLÉ

We serve this dish at lunchtime as a main course with a dressed green salad. We find it easiest to make two soufflés in 570ml/1 pint soufflé moulds. You can use one large mould, but the soufflé will take 10 minutes longer to cook, or use four ramekins, which will require 10 minutes less to cook, though the smaller soufflés will not stay risen for quite so long after they are cooked.

SERVES 4

65g/2½oz butter, plus 1 tablespoon for greasing

110g/4 oz onions, finely chopped

75g/3oz finely grated Parmesan

40g/1½oz plain flour

250ml/9fl oz milk

⅓ nutmeg, grated

85g/3½oz Gruyère cheese

4 egg yolks

2 tablespoons chopped chives

110g/4oz lean boiled ham, cut into 1cm/½in dice

5 egg whites

a pinch of cream of tartar or a few drops of lemon juice

flaked sea salt

freshly ground black pepper

Preheat the oven to 180C/350F/Gas 4.

Melt 25g/1oz of the butter in a pan over a medium heat with a couple of tablespoons of water and a pinch of salt. Add the onions and cook gently until they are soft but not coloured. Set aside.

Grease the soufflé moulds with butter using a brush and dust the insides with the Parmesan. Stand them in a deep roasting tin and set aside.

Melt the remaining 40g/1½oz butter in a pan over a moderate heat and whisk in the flour. Cook for a few minutes without browning, whisking regularly. Put this roux on one side to cool. Bring the milk to the boil in another pan, and season lightly with salt, pepper and nutmeg. Add the cooled roux, whisking continuously until it becomes a smooth but thick sauce. Remove from heat and, with a wooden spoon, beat in the Gruyère cheese and then the egg yolks. Stir in the chives, ham and reserved onions.

Whisk the egg whites with a pinch of cream of tartar or a few drops of lemon juice until they form soft peaks. Whisk a third of the egg whites into the cheese mixture to loosen it, and then pour the loosened mixture into the remaining egg whites, folding it in delicately with a large metal spoon. Divide the mixture between the moulds.

Pour enough boiling water into the roasting tin to come halfway up the moulds. Simmer for a few minutes on top of the stove, then transfer the tin to the oven and cook on the bottom shelf for 25–30 minutes. To test if the soufflés are cooked, insert the blade of a small knife and if it comes out clean, they are ready. Serve at once. **HM**

LEEK AND GOATS' CHEESE FILO PARCELS

SERVES 8 AS A FIRST COURSE

1kg/2lb 2oz leeks, cut into 3cm/1½in strips, washed and drained

100g/4oz caster sugar

grated zest and juice of 1 unwaxed lemon

100g/4oz soft goats' cheese

1 garlic clove, finely chopped

50g/2oz sliced hazelnuts

24 sheets of filo pastry, each about 23cm/9in square

150g/5oz melted butter

½ teaspoon caraway seeds

flaked sea salt

freshly ground black pepper

Place the leeks, sugar, lemon zest and juice in a pan, cover and stir over a low heat until the leeks are just cooked. Drain and allow the mixture to cool slightly. Add the cheese, garlic and hazelnuts, and season to taste.

Preheat the oven to 180C/350F/Gas 4. Grease a baking tray with butter.

Brush 3 sheets of the filo pastry lightly with butter. Layer them to make a star shape. Put a tablespoon of the mixture in the centre of the pastry. Draw the pastry up and over the mixture to make a parcel and twist closely to form a seal. Arrange the surplus pastry above the seal in a petal-like shape. Repeat until there are 8 parcels. Drizzle the parcels with butter and sprinkle with the caraway seeds. Place on the prepared tray and bake for 10–15 minutes until golden and crisp. **AB**

SMOKED BACON, SAUSAGE AND CHEESE ROLL WITH ORLY SAUCE

The flavours of this can be varied, depending upon the sausage meat and cheese that you use. Lincolnshire, lamb, pork or game sausage meat all work well; we use Chewton Mature Cheddar cheese, but any strong-flavoured Cheddar will do. The Orly sauce is very versatile: you can add saffron, pesto, basil, oregano, chillies, olives or anchovy purée to serve it with fish, chicken or vegetable dishes.

SERVES 8–10 AS A FIRST COURSE, AND 6 AS A SUPPER DISH

50g/2oz butter

250g/9oz onions, finely chopped

110g/4oz rindless streaky smoked bacon rashers

25g/1oz chopped parsley

250g/9oz mature Cheddar cheese, coarsely grated

450g/1lb sausage meat

450g/1lb ready-made puff pastry

1 egg, beaten

flaked sea salt

freshly ground black pepper

flour for dredging

FOR THE ORLY SAUCE

150g/6oz butter

2 tablespoons olive oil

4 garlic cloves, finely chopped

1 onion, finely chopped

1 celery stick, finely diced

1 medium carrot, finely diced

110g/4oz rindless smoked streaky bacon rashers, cut into 5mm/¼in dice

1½ tablespoons plain flour

1 tablespoon tomato purée

1 tablespoon caster sugar

275ml/½ pint white or brown chicken stock (see pages 27 and 28)

1kg/2lb 4oz vine-ripened tomatoes, diced, or 850g/1lb 12oz tinned chopped tomatoes

1 sprig fresh, or ½ teaspoon dried, thyme

1 bay leaf

12 black peppercorns

3 tablespoons chopped parsley

To make the filling for the roll, melt the butter and cook the onions until they are soft without letting them colour. Meanwhile, cut the bacon rashers into small strips. Add these to the onions and cook for a further few minutes. Transfer the mixture to a large bowl to cool. Mix in the parsley, half the grated cheese, the sausage meat and season with pepper (but no salt). Set aside.

Roll out the puff pastry on a well-floured surface and trim to make a rectangle of about 60 x 20cm/24 x 7½in. Transfer to a baking tray and cover with a kitchen towel or clingfilm to prevent it from drying, and rest in the refrigerator for about 40 minutes.

Preheat the oven to 180C/350F/Gas 4.

On a floured surface, shape the sausage filling into a roll about 60cm/24in long and lay this along the centre of the pastry. Sprinkle the remaining grated cheese over the sausage.

Beat the egg with a pinch of salt, and brush this over the exposed pastry. Wrap the pastry over the filling, pressing lightly to seal the edges together. Brush the pastry roll with egg and cut it in half. Lift the rolls on to a baking tray, and cook in the oven for 20–25 minutes, until the pastry is golden.

To make the sauce, melt 75g/3oz of the butter with the olive oil, and cook the garlic, onion, celery, carrot and bacon over a medium heat for 10–15 minutes. Stir in the flour, tomato purée and sugar and cook for another minute. Turn down the heat, add the rest of the ingredients and cook slowly for about an hour until the sauce thickens. Liquidise in a food processor, strain, and season to taste. (At this stage the sauce can be cooled and stored in the refrigerator for a few days if required.) Shortly before serving, reheat the sauce and stir in the remaining butter.

To serve, cut the rolls into slices about 3cm/1¼in thick, and hand the Orly sauce separately. **HM**

HARTINGTON QUICHE

The quiche can be made up to 3 days in advance. For every 12 servings, you will need a 30cm/12in loose-bottomed metal flan tin.

	NUMBER OF SERVINGS	
	12	48
FOR THE PASTRY		
plain flour	1kg/2lb	4kg/8lb
salt	1 level teaspoon	4 teaspoons
cold butter, cut into small pieces	220g/8oz	880g/2lb
cold lard, cut into small pieces`	220g/8oz	880g/2lb
cold water	5 teaspoons	20 teaspoons
FOR THE FILLING		
full-fat cream cheese	350g/14oz	1.7kg/3lb 8oz
double cream	500ml/1 pint	2l/4 pints
eggs	6	24
parsley, chopped	1 teaspoon	1 tablespoon
chives, chopped	1 teaspoon	1 tablespoon
Stilton cheese, with rind removed, grated	220g/8oz	880g/2lb
salt	a good pinch	½ teaspoon
white pepper	¼ teaspoon	1 teaspoon

To make the pastry, sift the flour and salt together and either mix them with the butter and lard in a food processor, or rub in the butter and lard with your fingertips until the mixture resembles fine breadcrumbs. Add the water either through the lid of the processor while it is running or, if you are making it by hand, gradually, using a knife to mix it in. Stop as soon as the dough holds together. Wrap in clingfilm and chill. Grease the tin/s.

Roll out the pastry on a floured surface to about 5mm/¼in thick and use it to line the tins. Be careful not to stretch the pastry. Trim off any excess by running the rolling pin over the top of the tin/s. There is no need to bake blind.

Preheat the oven to 190C/375F/Gas 5. Beat the cream cheese in a large mixing bowl with a little of the cream to loosen it. Beat in the eggs and then slowly add the remaining cream. Stir in the herbs and seasoning. Sprinkle the Stilton evenly over the pastry base/s. Pour in the filling and bake in the oven for 35–45 minutes, but check after 30 minutes. The quiche is done when the filling does not move if gently shaken and is golden brown on top. It can be served hot or cold. **PG**

LENTIL AND RED PEPPER BAKE

SERVES 8 AS A SUPPER OR LUNCH DISH

250g/9oz couscous	1 garlic clove, crushed
1 teaspoon ground cumin	200g/7oz grated cheese
500g/1lb split lentils	2 teaspoons tomato purée
50g/2oz butter	1 egg, beaten
200g/7oz onions, diced	flaked sea salt
200g/7oz red pepper slices	freshly ground black pepper

Pour the couscous into a bowl and add enough boiling water just to cover it. Add the cumin, season with salt and pepper and stir with a fork to break up any lumps. Leave until the couscous has absorbed all the water. Spoon into a 20cm/8in greased flan tin.

Wash the lentils, place them in a pan and just cover with cold water. Bring to the boil and simmer, uncovered, for 20–30 minutes until all the water has been absorbed. Stir continuously towards the end of the cooking time to prevent the mixture sticking – it should be as dry as possible.

Preheat the oven to 180C/350F/Gas 4.

Melt the butter over a medium heat and add the onions, red pepper slices and garlic. Fry gently for about 5 minutes. Remove from the heat and mix in the cooked lentils, grated cheese, tomato purée, beaten egg and salt and pepper. Spoon this over the couscous, level, and bake for about 45 minutes. **AB**

CHICKEN LIVER PÂTÉ WITH ONION, TOMATO AND COURGETTE CHUTNEY

This dish needs to be started at least three days ahead. In fact, is best made a week or so before it is eaten The pâté can be kept for up to two weeks in the fridge. The chutney will keep for a year or more, the flavour improving with age.

SERVES 12–24 AS A FIRST COURSE OR AS A SUPPER DISH

400g/14 oz chicken livers

500ml/1 pint milk

4 bay leaves

800g/1lb 12oz fresh belly of pork, without the rind, cut into 2cm/¾in dice

3 shallots

2–3 garlic cloves

40g/1½oz parsley, with stalks removed, chopped

1 small egg, beaten

1 sprig fresh, or ½ teaspoon dried, thyme

½ teaspoon four-spices

1 teaspoon grated nutmeg

4 juniper berries, lightly crushed

55ml/2fl oz double cream

55ml/2fl oz Madeira

25ml/1fl oz brandy

25ml/1fl oz rum

12g/½oz salt for every 900g/2lb of mixture

1 teaspoon ground pepper for every 900g/2lb of mixture

2 eating apples, peeled, cored and cut into 1cm/½in dice

200g/7oz rindless streaky bacon rashers, to cover pâté

150g/5oz clarified butter

FOR THE CHUTNEY

450g/1lb onions, cut in half and sliced

150g/5oz tomatoes, diced but not skinned

150g/5oz courgettes, sliced but not peeled

1 large garlic clove, crushed

200g/7oz caster sugar

40g/1½oz sultanas

1 tablespoon grated fresh ginger

1 tablespoon flaked sea salt

1 teaspoon freshly ground black pepper

450ml/16fl oz red wine vinegar

Start by cleaning the chicken livers. Remove any small green (bitter) pockets of gall bladder or green discolouration, but be careful not to pierce the livers. Leave the livers to soak in the milk with 2 of the bay leaves for 24 hours (this process helps to prevent bitterness).

The next day, preheat the oven to 180C/350F/Gas 4. Rinse the chicken livers in cold water and drain. Coarsely mince the livers, pork, shallots, garlic and parsley. (You can use a food processor for this, but the texture of the end result will not be as coarse.) Add the egg, thyme, spices, juniper berries, cream, Madeira, brandy and rum. Then weigh the mixture to work out the amount of seasoning needed, and add as appropriate. Mix in the diced apples, stirring everything together well.

Arrange the remaining 2 bay leaves in the bottom of a terrine mould or loaf tin (about 28 x 10cm/11 x 4in and 7cm/3in deep). Spoon in the pâté mixture, level it, and lay the bacon rashers over the top. Cover with a lid or foil, stand in a deep roasting tin and pour in enough boiling water to come at least halfway up the sides of the terrine. Cook in the oven for 1¼ hours, checking the water level from time to time. Remove the lid or foil to allow the surface of the pâté to colour, and cook for a further 15 minutes.

Check that the pâté is cooked: if the juices are clear, the pâté is ready. If not, cook for a further 10–15 minutes. Take the terrine out of the roasting tin, but before it cools, press the pâté to allow the hot juices to rise to the surface. This will keep it moist, prevent it from discolouring and help to keep it firm for slicing. We press the pâté by wrapping foil round a thin piece of wood that fits just inside a terrine mould and weighing it down with four 1kg/2lb weights (you could use a loaf tin weighed down with 4 or 5 tins of tomatoes).

Once the pâté is cold, remove the weights, melt the butter and pour a layer on top of the pâté. Refrigerate for several days to let the flavours develop.

To make the chutney, place all ingredients in a pan and bring to the boil. Turn the heat down and simmer very gently for about 40 minutes or until the mixture resembles a paste. Cool, pour into sterilized jars, cover with lids and refrigerate. HM

'DARLING BUDD' TERRINE

Margaret Budd gave me the receipt for this excellent terrine which goes like a bomb in the Farm Shop, where it is called 'Darling Budd' of course. Her husband served in the same RAF squadron as Pam's husband Derek. Bound by their interest in their kitchens, the two women made a lasting friendship. Margaret comes to us for alternate Christmases. Her company and her advice on food are invaluable to me. **DD**

SERVES 10

450g/1lb belly of pork, coarsely minced

225g/8oz best pork sausage meat

a small glass of red wine

225g/8oz chicken livers, cleaned (see top of page 71) and roughly chopped

225g/8oz bacon, finely chopped

1 garlic clove, finely chopped

12 juniper berries, lightly crushed

1 teaspoon chopped fresh, or ½ teaspoon dried, thyme

100g/4oz streaky bacon rashers, to cover pâté

Preheat the oven to 180C/350F/Gas 4.

Mix together all the ingredients except the bacon rashers and place in a buttered, earthenware terrine mould (9 x 20cm/3½ x 8in and 7cm/3in deep). Cover the top with the streaky bacon. Cover the mould with a lid or foil, stand it in a roasting tin and pour in enough boiling water to come halfway up the sides of the mould. Cook in the oven for 1½ hours, removing the lid or foil after an hour to allow the surface of the pâté to colour. Check the water level in the roasting tin at the same time.

To make sure the pâté is thoroughly cooked, probe the centre with a metal skewer and leave it there for 10 seconds; when you remove the skewer, the end should be hot. If not, leave for another 15 minutes. Once it is cooked, take the pâté out of the oven and allow it to cool before refrigerating overnight. **AB**

ARIZONA DESERT SALAD

Candida Lycett-Green, as brilliant at cooking as she is at driving a coloured horse to a flat cart over the Berkshire Downs, produced this for lunch when I was staying near Faringdon. I asked her if I could use it in this book, 'It's Nicky Haslam's. He met it in Arizona. Ask Nicky.' she said. He allowed it, so here it is. I had three helpings in Candida's house and my eight- and nine-year old Morrison grandchildren follow suit now that it is a regular here. DD

SERVES 6 AS A SUPPER OR LUNCH DISH

3 celery hearts, small leafy sticks only

150g/5oz radishes, topped, tailed and sliced

3 shallots or 12 spring onions (or a mixture of both), finely diced

1 garlic clove, finely chopped

2 tablespoons chopped parsley

2 tablespoons chopped chives

2 tablespoons chopped chervil

75ml/3fl oz olive oil

2 tablespoons truffle oil

2 tablespoons white wine vinegar

12 frankfurter sausages

800g/1lb 12oz pink fir potatoes (or any good salad potatoes), unpeeled

flaked sea salt

freshly ground black pepper

Roughly chop the leaves of the celery and slice the sticks. Combine the celery, radishes, shallots or spring onions, garlic and herbs in a large bowl. Add the oils and vinegar, and mix well. Cook the potatoes and skin them when they are cool enough to handle. Cut each potato in half and add to the salad while still warm. Cook the frankfurter sausages for about 5 minutes, either by dry-frying them or grilling them. Cut each into 3 and add to the salad. Toss everything together and season generously with salt and pepper. Either serve immediately when warm, or leave to cool and serve cold. **DW**

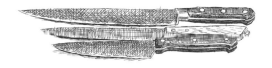

CRAB, LOBSTER AND GRUYÈRE TART

You can make the pastry cases 5 days in advance, and cook the leeks a day ahead. Uncooked lobster tails are available deep frozen; defrost and use them raw. For every 12 servings, you will need a 30cm/12in loose-bottomed flan tin.

	NUMBER OF SERVINGS	
	12	48
FOR THE PASTRY		
plain flour	170g/6oz	680g/1lb 8oz
salt	1 level teaspoon	4 teaspoons
cold butter, cut into small pieces	85g/3oz	340g/12oz
cold lard, cut into small pieces`	45g/1½oz	180g/6oz
cold water	70ml/2½fl oz	280ml/½ pint
FOR THE FILLING		
butter	50g/2oz	200g/8oz
leeks, washed, finely sliced	180g/6oz	720g/1lb 8oz
lobster tails, cut into slices	240g/8oz	960g/2lb
egg yolks	6	24
double cream	240ml/½ pint	960ml/2 pints
white crabmeat, cooked	660g/1lb 8oz	2.6kg/6lb
Gruyère cheese, grated	180g/6oz	720g/1lb 8oz
cayenne pepper for dusting		
flaked sea salt		
freshly ground pepper		

To make the pastry, sift the flour and salt together, and either mix them with the butter and lard in a food processor, or rub in the butter and lard with your fingertips until the mixture resembles fine breadcrumbs. Add the water either through the lid of the processor while it is running or, if you are making it by hand, gradually, using a knife to mix it in. Stop as soon as the dough holds together. Wrap in clingfilm and chill. Grease the tin/s.

Preheat the oven to 180C/350F/Gas 4. Roll out the pastry on a well-floured surface to about 5mm/¼in thick and use it to line the tin/s. Be careful not to stretch the pastry. Trim off any excess by running the rolling pin over the top of the tin/s. Bake blind (line the flan with greaseproof paper and weight the paper with baking beans) for 15 minutes. Remove the baking beans and paper, and leave the pastry case/s to cool.

To make the filling, start by melting the butter in a pan and cooking the leeks for 3 minutes until they are soft but not coloured. Set aside.

When you are ready to assemble the tart, preheat the oven to 180C/350F/Gas 4.

Season the pastry base with salt and pepper, distribute the leeks over the pastry and arrange the lobster on top of the leeks. Whisk the egg yolks and cream together, season with salt and pepper, and fold in the crabmeat. Pour into the pastry cases and cover with the grated Gruyère cheese and a dusting of cayenne pepper. Bake in the oven for 20 minutes or until the filling has set and the cheese is golden brown.

Let the tart/s cool slightly before cutting, or they will break up, though they are best served warm. **PG**

SALMON GRAVLAX AND CHEDDAR TERRINE WITH BEURRE BLANC SAUCE

This dish takes 4 days to complete if you choose to make the gravlax. You can make it with bought gravlax, in which case it will take 2 days to complete. Once made, the terrine will keep for 4–5 days in the fridge. The sauce can be made 2 or 3 hours in advance, and kept warm. For every 12 servings, you will need a terrine mould or loaf tin measuring about 30 x 10cm/12 x 4in and 7.5cm/3in deep.

	NUMBER OF SERVINGS	
	12	48
FOR THE SALMON GRAVLAX		
salmon fillet, skinned and any bones removed	500g/1lb 2oz	2kg/4lb 8oz
sea salt, coarse	60g/2oz	240g/8oz
sugar	60g/2oz	240g/8oz
white peppercorns, crushed	45g/1½oz	180g/5oz
fresh dill, with stalks on	45g/1½oz	180g/5oz
brandy	30ml/1½fl oz	150ml/¼ pint
olive oil	30ml/1½fl oz	150ml/¼ pint
FOR THE TERRINE		
salmon gravlax (see above)	500g/1lb 2oz	2kg/4lb 8oz
mature Cheddar cheese, cut into small cubes	500g/1lb 2oz	2kg/4lb 8oz
Gewürztraminer white wine	1l/1¾ pints	4l/7 pints
dry-cured streaky bacon	20 rashers	80 rashers
garlic cloves, finely chopped	6	24
waxy potatoes, soft boiled and thinly sliced	20	80
whole eggs	3	12
egg yolks	3	12
double cream	500ml/1¼ pints	2l/5 pints
flaked sea salt		
freshly ground black pepper		
clarified butter (optional), for pan-frying	150g/6oz	600g/1lb 8oz

FOR THE BEURRE BLANC SAUCE

shallots, chopped finely	225g/5oz	900g/1lb 4oz
lemons, juice of	1½	6
double cream	125ml/¼ pint	500ml/1 pint
cold water	125ml/¼ pint	500ml/1 pint
butter, cut into small cubes	675g/1lb 8oz	2.7kg/6lb
flaked sea salt		
freshly ground pepper		

Start preparing the gravlax 2 days before you want to make the terrine. Cut the salmon (in one piece) to the shape and size to fit the terrine mould and discard the skin. Combine the salt, sugar and white peppercorns. Bruise the dill stalks. Take a large sheet of clingfilm, lay a little bruised dill on this, then the single layer of salmon, sprinkle with some salt mixture, and then drizzle over a little brandy and olive oil. Fold over the clingfilm to seal. Wrap in another sheet of clingfilm. Place the salmon parcel in the mould and weigh it down by placing another dish or loaf tin on top, three-quarters-full of water. (If you are making this in large quantities, you will need to make more than one clingfilm package of salmon and fill further terrine moulds.) Leave for 6 hours, then turn the salmon over and weigh it down again. Leave overnight. Turn again twice the following day and keep it weighed down.

A day before you make the terrine, put the Cheddar cheese to marinate in the white wine for 24 hours

When you are ready to make the terrine, preheat the oven to 150C/300F/Gas 2.

If you are using bought gravlax, which usually comes in thin slices like smoked salmon, layer the slices to make a shape and size similar to the terrine. If you have made the gravlax, unwrap it and scrape off the excess marinade.

Line each terrine mould with 4 layers of clingfilm, leaving an overhang of 20cm/8in on each side. Line the bottom and sides with the bacon rashers, leaving an overhang for wrapping over the top when the terrine is full. Drain the cheese and put a layer the bottom of the mould. Cover with some of the garlic and season with salt and pepper. Add a layer of potato slices. Then cover the potato with the salmon. Continue to layer the terrine with the cheese, garlic and seasoning, and potato slices until the mould is full.

Whisk the eggs and yolks lightly, then whisk in the cream and season with salt and pepper. Pour this into the terrine. Pull the overhanging strips of bacon over the top of the terrine and wrap over the layers of clingfilm tightly to seal the top of the terrine. Stand the terrine in a roasting tin and pour in enough boiling water to come halfway up the sides of the terrine. Cook in the oven for 1¼ hours. Cool, place the weight on top and refrigerate for 12 hours or overnight.

To make the sauce, place the shallots in a pan with the lemon juice and cook over a medium heat until the juice is reduced by 90 per cent, and the shallots are soft but almost dry. Stir in the cream and cold water. Return to the heat. Add the butter a few cubes at a time, whisking them in as they melt – do not allow the sauce to boil. Season with a little pepper. Set aside and keep warm.

Shortly before serving, take the terrine out of its mould, unwrap the clingfilm and slice. Either pan-fry the slices in the clarified butter for a minute on each side, or put them on hot plates and put these in a warm oven for 1–2 minutes to soften the cheese before drizzling over the sauce. **PG**

FISH

&

SHELLFISH

'I T'S NOT THE PRICE THAT MAKES THE DISH. The herring is the
king of fish,' my mother used to intone whenever the shining example
of her economical housekeeping appeared. It was true. But where are the
herrings? Where are the hard and soft roes which used to decorate their
grilled parents, and what's the point of mustard sauce now? Fish have
turned upside down, belly up, in the last few years. It's incredible to me
that salmon (albeit nasty pale stuff) is cheaper than cod and that the
once-dreaded food of schools, hospitals and prisons is now a luxury.

When I was fourteen, Decca (two and a half years older) left home for
Paris to learn French. A governess for me alone was thought to be too
extravagant, so it had to be school. The supper provided on the second of
the two frightful nights I spent at a weekly boarding school was a huge pile
of cod dressed in black skin. It was the last straw. I couldn't understand the
lessons, nor the rules of lacrosse, and I fainted in geometry. But it is the
cod supper that sticks in the memory, as it did in the gullet.

The term started on a Wednesday so, thankfully, by Friday I was at
home and telling my mother that nothing would induce me to go back.
Having paid for the term in advance she insisted that I stick it out as a
day girl, travelling to and fro Oxford from Shipton-under-Wychwood in
the dark winter mornings and evenings by train on good old GWR, third
class with no rapists or murderers. There was much tut-tutting from
aunts and others who thought my mother's indulgence was too spoiling.
'It will be the ruination of that child.' But I am ever grateful to her.

Our attempts at schools seem to have been mixed up with food.
Several years earlier, when we lived at High Wycombe and our governess
had left suddenly and under a cloud, Decca and I tried the rest of that
term at a day school in Beaconsfield. The lunch was so horrible that we
persuaded our father to go and see the headmistress about it. I wish I had
been at that interview, as two formidable characters faced each other
about two fussy children's lunches. Our father won and we were allowed
to take bananas from home, which we ate in a passage. My parents could
be relied upon when it came to the crunch and the crunch was lunch. DD

LADY GAGE'S SMOKED HADDOCK À LA CRÈME

Diana Gage was a cousin of Andrew's, born Cavendish, of wonderful Holker Hall between the Lakes and the sea. She was one of several sisters who returned to cottages near their old home after they were widowed to cook and garden to their hearts' content and to the delight of their friends. Her two receipts in this book (see also page 199) are from Food From Firle *written when she was married to George Gage and lived at Firle Place, their Sussex house built of pale Caen stone under the downs near Lewes.* **DD**

We serve this dish for supper with steamed new potatoes sprinkled with chopped chives.

SERVES 6

6 undyed smoked haddock fillets, each weighing about 200g/8oz, skinned, any bones removed, and cut into 25g/1oz cubes

cayenne pepper
freshly ground black pepper
570ml/1 pint double cream

Preheat the oven to 200C/400F/Gas 6.

Cover the haddock with cold water in a pan and bring just to boiling point. Immediately take it off the heat and strain. Put the fish into a gratin dish, sprinkle with a little cayenne and black pepper and cover with the cream. Place the dish on a tray to catch any cream that boils over and bake for about 20 minutes. The haddock is ready when a thin brown skin forms and the cream is reduced to a thin coating sauce. **HM**

SEA BASS FILLETS IN PASTRY WITH BÉARNAISE SAUCE

SERVES 6

8 sea bass fillets, each weighing
   about 85g/3½oz, any bones
   removed, but with the skin on
55ml/2fl oz warmed clarified butter,
   or vegetable oil
450g/1lb ready-made puff pastry
flour for dredging
1 egg, beaten with a pinch of salt
flaked sea salt
freshly ground black pepper

FOR THE STUFFING
50g/2oz butter
80g/3oz shallots, finely chopped
2 garlic cloves, finely chopped
4 medium vine-ripened tomatoes,
   skinned, deseeded and diced
1 teaspoon tomato purée
250g/9oz white mushrooms, chopped
   to the texture of rock salt
55ml/2fl oz double cream

juice of ½ lemon
110g/4oz clarified butter
110g/4oz fresh white breadcrumbs
2 hard-boiled eggs, coarsely grated
110g/4oz boiled ham slices, cut into
   1cm/½in dice
1 tablespoon chopped fresh tarragon
1 tablespoon chopped parsley

FOR THE BÉARNAISE SAUCE
8 black peppercorns, lightly crushed
40g/1½oz shallots, finely chopped
55ml/2fl oz tarragon or white wine
   vinegar
55ml/2fl oz dry white wine
3 tablespoons chopped fresh tarragon
3 egg yolks
200ml/7fl oz warmed clarified butter
1 tablespoon chopped parsley
1 tablespoon chopped chervil

Start by making the stuffing. Melt the butter over a low heat, add the shallots and garlic and cook until soft without letting them brown. Divide the mixture between two pans. To one pan, add the diced tomatoes and tomato purée, turn up the heat and cook until all the moisture has evaporated. Set aside. To the other pan, add the mushrooms and turn up the heat and again cook until all the juices have evaporated, stirring continuously to prevent sticking. Add the cream and lemon juice.

Continue to cook until the cream has been absorbed into the mixture. Season to taste, and set aside. Melt the clarified butter over a medium heat, add the breadcrumbs and fry until golden and crisp, tossing to prevent them burning. Strain off the clarified butter and, while the crumbs are still warm, season with a pinch of salt. Now mix together the tomato and mushroom purées, the fried crumbs, grated hard-boiled eggs, diced boiled ham and chopped herbs. You should have a stiff but moist mixture. Season to taste.

Prepare the sea bass fillets by seasoning them on both sides. Melt the warmed clarified butter in, or pour the vegetable oil into, a large frying pan over a high heat. Fry the fillets for a minute on each side to seal, but not cook, them. Lift them on to a cold tray to cool. Save any juices from the tray and add them to the stuffing.

Roll out the pastry and trim to a neat oblong of 46 x 40cm/18 x 16in. Dredge both sides with flour to avoid sticking. Place a third of the stuffing in the centre of the pastry along the length, covering an area of about 30 x 10cm/12 x 4in. Lay 4 sea bass fillets on top. Repeat these layers, finishing with the remaining third of the stuffing.

Brush the exposed pastry with the beaten egg. Using both hands, wrap the pastry over the filling without stretching it, and seal the long edge. Using a rolling pin, and rolling away from the filling, thin out the short ends of the pastry. Trim neatly, leaving enough pastry to fold the ends under. Lift the pastry roll on to a baking tray, seam-side down, and tuck under the ends. Brush the top with beaten egg and make a few holes along the top of the pastry to allow steam to escape. Refrigerate for 20 minutes to rest the pastry.

Preheat the oven to 180C/350F/Gas 4.

Make the Béarnaise sauce by combining the peppercorns, shallots, vinegar, white wine and 1 tablespoon of the chopped tarragon in a small heavy-bottomed pan. Bring these to the boil and simmer until almost all the liquid has evaporated. Transfer the reduction to a bowl and leave to cool. In the same pan, but off the heat, whisk the egg yolks and 55ml/2fl oz of water to a foam. Put the pan over a very low heat and continue to whisk until the mixture is a light, creamy consistence and the whisk leaves ribbon-like trails when it is lifted. Take off the heat and gradually whisk in the clarified butter. Stir in the reduction and the remaining herbs and season to taste with salt and pepper.

Bake the sea bass roll for 45 minutes.

To serve, cut into slices, overlapping these on a warmed serving dish. Hand the Béarnaise sauce separately. HM

SALMON PICCATAS WITH SORREL SAUCE

Much of the preparation, including making the sauce, can be done a day ahead and kept in the refrigerator, but the fish does require last-minute cooking.

SERVES 6

about 6 tablespoons vegetable oil
900g/2lb salmon fillet (thick end only) skinless, any bones removed, and cut into 18 straight slices
flaked sea salt
freshly ground black pepper

FOR THE SORREL SAUCE
75g/3oz butter
125g/4½ oz sorrel leaves, washed (left whole if young, and with stalks removed and cut into strips if older)
75g/3oz shallots, finely sliced
200ml/7fl oz Noilly-Prat
570ml/1 pint fish stock (see page 29)
1 tablespoon black peppercorns, lightly crushed
270ml/½ pint double cream

To make the sauce, start by melting 25g/1oz of the butter in a pan over a medium heat. Add the sorrel and stew for a few minutes until it has wilted. Set it aside to cool. Put the shallots, Noilly-Prat, fish stock and peppercorns in a pan, bring them to the boil and continue to boil until the mixture is reduced to about 150ml/¼ pint. Add the cream and boil for about another 5 minutes. Strain this into a clean pan through a fine sieve, pressing with the back of a spoon to make sure as much of the sauce goes through as possible. Bring back to the boil and simmer until the sauce thickens to a coating consistency. Then add the sorrel. Check the consistency, as the sorrel juices will thin the sauce, and reduce further as necessary. Take off the heat, cover and keep warm.

Start preparing the salmon piccatas by cutting out twelve 23cm/9in squares of silicone paper. (These squares are used to minimise handling the fish once it has been batted out to make a 'piccata', when it is very delicate.) Using a brush, thinly coat one side of each square with oil. Season both sides of the salmon slices with salt and pepper. Place one square of silicone paper, oil-side up, on a chopping board and put 3 salmon slices on it, leaving about 2cm/¾in between each slice. Cover with another square of silicone paper, oil-side down. With the flat side of a knife, gently bat out the slices until they are about 5mm/¼in thick. (Three batted-out slices of fish form one portion.) Set aside and repeat the process with the remaining salmon.

When you are ready to cook the salmon, heat up 1½ tablespoons of the oil until hot in a frying pan (non-stick if possible) that is large enough to contain at least one portion. Peel off the top square of silicone paper and, retaining the bottom square of paper intact, quickly place the piccatas, fish-side down, in the pan and peel off the remaining sheet of paper. Fry for a few seconds, turn the piccatas over, and flash-fry again so both sides are lightly browned and crisp. Lift on to a serving dish and keep warm. Repeat the process with the other portions, changing the oil when you have cooked three.

To serve, reheat the sauce, stir in the remaining butter and pour over the fish. **HM**

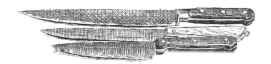

ROAST MONKFISH 'NOT QUITE CUBAT'

This dish is a variation on traditional 'Cubat', which involves mushroom purée and Mornay sauce garnished with truffles. Our version includes the mushroom purée, but uses a simpler, lemon butter sauce.

SERVES 6

6 single monkfish fillets, each
  weighing about 175g/6oz (ask your
  fishmonger to remove the sticky
  skin)
150g/5oz clarified butter
flaked sea salt
freshly ground black pepper

FOR THE MUSHROOM PURÉE
900g/2lb white mushrooms
150g/5oz butter
150g/5oz shallots, finely chopped
2 garlic cloves, finely chopped
juice of 1 lemon

2 tablespoons double cream
1 tablespoon chopped parsley
1 tablespoon chopped fresh tarragon

FOR THE LEMON BUTTER
SAUCE
juice of 1 lemon
110ml/4fl oz double cream
300g/10oz cold unsalted butter,
  cut into 1cm/½in squares
2 tablespoons chopped chives

First, make mushroom purée. Chop the mushrooms until they are the texture of rock salt. Alternatively, you can use a food processor, but blend only small quantities at a time, turning the machine on and off so that the mushrooms do not become liquidised.

Melt the butter over a moderate heat, add the shallots and garlic and cook them, without letting them brown, until they are soft. (Adding a tablespoon or two of water and a pinch of salt will help to avoid browning.) Add the mushrooms, season lightly, and turn up the heat and cook until all the juices have evaporated, stirring continuously to prevent sticking. Add the lemon juice, cream and herbs. Cook for a further 3–4 minutes until the cream has been absorbed, adjust the seasoning, and set aside to keep warm.

Preheat the oven to 200C/400F/Gas 6.

Prepare the monkfish by cutting each fillet in half, and season each piece with salt and pepper. In a shallow roasting tray large enough to hold the fish, heat the clarified butter until very hot and fry the fillets on both sides until they are brown. Put the dish in the oven and roast for 7–8 minutes or until milky juices set on the surface of the fish.

Make the lemon butter sauce while the fish is cooking. Bring the lemon juice, cream and 110ml/4fl oz of water to the boil and reduce slightly. Add all the butter and whisk continuously until it is well blended. Take off the heat, add the chives, and season with salt and pepper to taste. Keep the sauce warm but do not let it boil.

To serve, arrange the monkfish over the mushroom purée and ladle over a little sauce, reserving most of the sauce to hand separately. **HM**

FISHCAKES WITH CAPER AND ANCHOVY MAYONNAISE

SERVES 6 (3 PER PERSON)

220g/8oz salmon fillets, skinned and
   any bones removed
220g/8oz white fish (cod, haddock or
   whiting), skinned and any bones
   removed
1 sprig fresh, or ½ teaspoon dried,
   thyme
1 bay leaf
450g/1lb potatoes, cut into even
   pieces, each weighing about 50g/2oz
65g/2½oz butter
55g/2oz shallots, finely chopped
1 garlic clove, finely chopped
1 tablespoon chopped parsley
1 tablespoon chopped fresh coriander
   leaves
2 tablespoons finely chopped chives
   or spring onions
½ teaspoon dried chilli flakes
4 teaspoons grated fresh ginger
½ teaspoon grated nutmeg
a splash of Tabasco sauce
1 tablespoon Worcestershire sauce
6 anchovy fillets in oil, finely diced
oil for deep frying, or 200ml/7fl oz
   clarified butter or oil for sautéing

flaked sea salt
freshly ground black pepper
1 lemon, cut into 6 wedges

FOR CRUMBING
150g/5oz plain flour
200g/7oz fresh white breadcrumbs
2 tablespoons chopped parsley
2 eggs, beaten
75ml/3fl oz vegetable oil

FOR THE MAYONNAISE
1 egg yolk
1 tablespoon Dijon mustard
1 garlic clove, lightly crushed
110ml/4fl oz olive oil
150ml/5fl oz vegetable oil
1 tablespoon white wine or cider
   vinegar
1 tablespoon finely chopped capers
1 tablespoon finely chopped gherkins
3 tablespoons finely chopped parsley
6 pitted black olives, finely chopped
8 anchovy fillets in oil, puréed

Place the fish, thyme and bay leaf in a pan and cover with 570ml/1 pint of
lightly salted cold water. Bring to the boil, turn down the heat, cover, and

simmer for 3–4 minutes. Discard the thyme and bay leaf, lift the fish out and set it aside.

Put the potatoes into the poaching liquid. Bring to the boil, cover and simmer for 20 minutes, or until soft. Drain and return the potatoes to the pan.

Melt a g/¾oz of the butter in another small pan and cook the shallots and garlic for a few minutes until soft but not coloured. Add these to the potatoes with the parsley, coriander, chives or spring onions, chilli flakes, ginger, nutmeg, Tabasco and Worcestershire sauces, and the remaining butter. Mash coarsely, and add the anchovy fillets. Flake the poached fish and gently mix it into the potatoes so you do not up break the fish flakes. Season to taste. Allow to cool, cover with clingfilm and refrigerate.

Prepare the crumbing by whisking the eggs with the oil. Season well with salt and pepper. Put the flour on one tray and the breadcrumbs on another tray. Divide the fish mixture into 18 balls. Using a little flour to prevent the mixture sticking to your hands, roll the balls in the tray containing flour, then dip them into the whisked eggs, shaking off excess egg before coating them with breadcrumbs. Gently flatten each ball with a palette knife into a fishcake shape. Place on a tray, cover with clingfilm and refrigerate.

Before you start to make the mayonnaise, ensure that all the ingredients are at room temperature. Combine the oils. Whisk, or process, the egg yolk, mustard and garlic together. Then, whisking or processing continuously, add the oil very slowly, spoon by spoon, until the mayonnaise thickens and emulsifies. If it begins to separate, whisk 15ml/1 tablespoon of mayonnaise either with another egg yolk or, if you like a more fiery taste, with 15ml/1 tablespoon of mustard until creamy, then slowly whisk in the remaining mayonnaise. When two-thirds of the oil have been absorbed, whisk or process in the remaining oil in a steady flow. Whisk in the vinegar and a couple of tablespoons of boiling water to stabilise the emulsion. Discard the garlic if you have not used a processor. Season to taste and stir in the capers, gherkins, parsley, olives and anchovies.

If you use a deep fryer, heat it to 180C/350F, or put the clarified butter or vegetable oil into a large sauté pan over a medium heat. Deep fry or sauté the fishcakes for about 5 minutes until crisp and golden. Serve them accompanied by the lemon wedges, and hand the mayonnaise separately. HM

SEAFOOD BOMBE WITH SAFFRON SAUCE

When Pam was living in Ireland, I telephoned her one March morning to ask her to come over to Lismore. I got short shrift. 'No, of course, I can't,' she boomed down the line. 'I'm far too busy making egg mousse for sixty'. I had forgotten that it was the day of the Tipperary point-to-point. You would be far too busy to speak to anyone if you were making this seafood receipt for sixty – so complicated is it, with a layer of pink salmon wrapped round white fish which has already been made into a mousse; but Philip assures me that it is not difficult, and only a little practice is needed to make a perfect bombe. DD

The sauce can be made a day ahead, and the bombes several hours in advance.

	NUMBER OF SERVINGS	
	12	50
white fish (whiting or brill), skinned and any bones removed	120g/5oz	480g/1lb 4oz
egg whites	12	48
whipping cream	500ml/1 pint	2l/4 pints
lemons, juice of	½	2
salmon fillet, skinned and boned	720g/1lb 12oz	2.8kg/7lb
salt and pepper		

FOR THE SAFFRON SAUCE

butter	30g/1oz	110g/4oz
onions, finely chopped	250g/10oz	1kg/2lb 4oz
white wine	600ml/1¼ pints	2.4l/5 pints
peppercorns	4	16
bay leaves	1	4
fish stock (see page 29)	600ml/1¼ pints	2.4l/5 pints
beurre manié (equal parts of softened butter and flour mixed together to a paste)	60g/2oz	240g/8oz
double cream	600ml/1¼ pints	2.4l/5 pints
saffron	1 teaspoon	4 teaspoons

Start by making the mousse filling. Make sure there are no bones in the white fish, and then blend it until smooth. Add the egg whites. Whip the cream to soft peaks. Beat a quarter of the cream into the fish mixture. Gradually fold in the remainder of the cream, ensuring it is well combined. Add the lemon juice, season and mix well. Fill a piping bag with a plain, 1cm/½in nozzle.

Make the bombes by slicing the salmon into fine escalopes (i.e. into thin slices, cut at 45 degrees to the vertical) or ask your fishmonger to do this. Take two pieces of clingfilm, each 30cm/12in square, and place one on top of the other at a 45-degree angle. Season the clingfilm with salt and pepper. Weigh out about 60g/2½oz of the salmon slices and arrange them in the centre of the clingfilm to form a disc shape, making sure there are no gaps or holes between the pieces. Pipe 50g/2oz of the fish mousse in a ball on the middle of the salmon and season with salt and pepper. Being careful not to disrupt the salmon or mousse, lift the clingfilm into one hand, cupping your palm round it. With the other hand gently wrap the salmon over the mousse totally enclosing it. Pull the clingfilm over the top of the bombe tightly to keep the ball shape. Twist the clingfilm round, making sure there are no pockets of air. (Practice makes perfect – if you think it is not going to form a ball, take it apart and start again.) Repeat until all the fish is used.

Place the bombes in one layer in a steamer, and steam for 20 minutes. Transfer to a board, make a slit in the clingfilm and unwrap each bombe carefully. Place the bombes on a serving dish and keep warm.

While the bombes are steaming, make the sauce. Melt the butter in a pan over a gentle heat and add the onions. Cook until they are soft but not coloured. Add the wine, peppercorns and bay leaves. Turn up the heat and boil until the liquid has reduced by half. Then add fish stock. Bring to the boil. Add the beurre manié slowly and allow it to cook thoroughly, stirring all the time until it makes a smooth sauce.

In another pan, bring the cream to the boil, put in the saffron, take off the heat and let it infuse for a minute or two. Strain the fish sauce into the cream, and bring the sauce briefly back to the boil before serving. (If you make the sauce ahead of time, place clingfilm on the surface of the sauce to prevent a skin forming, and cool.) **PG**

SCALLOP AND MUSHROOM TERRINE WITH CLEMENCE SAUCE

Madame Clemence was a chef in a small restaurant in the Loire Valley near Nantes that specialised in fish dishes. One day she ran out of sauce and, in a panic, made do with the ingredients she had to hand. The result was this butter sauce; it impressed the customers so much that it became known in the Loire Valley as beurre blanc 'Nantais', *a name that has become shortened and known worldwide as Beurre Blanc.*

For the terrine you will need a mould or loaf tin about 26 x 12cm/10½ x 4½in and 6cm/2½in deep, or two smaller moulds, each 18 x 9cm/7 x 3½in and 5cm/2in deep. The terrine can be made 2–3 days in advance and reheated in its mould, in a bain-marie, for 35–40 minutes.

SERVES 6 AS A SUPPER DISH, OR 12 AS A FIRST COURSE

25g/1oz butter

juice of ½ lemon

200g/7oz white button mushrooms, finely sliced

50g/2oz soft butter for greasing

250g/9oz fresh scallops with roe, left whole

250g/9oz fresh scallops with roe, finely diced

250g/9oz haddock fillet, skinned and any bones removed, and cut into several pieces

3 egg whites

½ nutmeg, grated

425ml/¾ pint very cold double cream

2 tablespoons chopped chives

flaked sea salt

freshly ground black pepper

FOR THE PANADA

170ml/6fl oz milk

20g/¾oz butter

85g/3½oz strong plain flour

3 egg yolks

FOR THE BUTTER SAUCE

4 shallots, finely chopped

200ml/8fl oz dry white wine

200ml/8fl oz white wine vinegar

150ml/¼ pint double cream

350g/12oz cold butter, cut into 1cm/½in dice

Start by cooking the mushrooms. Bring 100ml/4fl oz of water, the 25g/1oz butter and the lemon juice to the boil with a pinch of salt. Add the mushrooms and cook, covered, for a few minutes until they are soft. Take off the heat, uncover and leave to cool. Then drain and squeeze out all the moisture.

Now make the panada. Bring the milk and butter to the boil, tip in the flour all at once and, using a wooden spoon, beat the mixture over a moderate heat for about one minute until it becomes a smooth paste and comes away from the sides of the pan. Transfer to a mixing bowl and leave it to stand for a few minutes to cool. Then beat in the egg yolks one by one, and beat until the paste is smooth again. Wrap the panada in clingfilm to avoid drying out and refrigerate until quite cold.

Preheat the oven to 180C/350F/Gas 4 and put a food processor bowl and blade in the freezer to get cold. Cut out a piece of greaseproof paper the size of the top of the terrine moulds or tins. Brush these and the inside of terrine mould or tins generously with the soft butter.

In the cold processor bowl, blend the whole scallops, the haddock pieces and egg whites until smooth. Add the cold panada, the nutmeg 1½ tablespoonfuls of salt, 1 teaspoonful of pepper and process again. Add the cream, a third at a time, but do not over-process because this will warm up the mixture. Transfer the mixture to a cold bowl and fold in the diced scallops, the mushrooms and one tablespoon of the chives. Spoon into the mould or tins and level evenly with a palette knife. Place the greaseproof paper on top, and seal with foil. Stand the mould or tins in a deep roasting tin, pour in enough boiling water to come halfway up their sides and bake in the oven for 45 minutes or until springy to the touch. Remove from the oven and allow to rest for at least 30 minutes in a warm spot.

Meanwhile make the sauce. In a non-aluminium pan, combine the shallots, wine and vinegar and cook over a medium heat until the liquid has evaporated and you are left with a thick purée. Add the cream and simmer until it has reduced by half. Now, little by little, whisk in the diced butter. Take off the heat, season to taste and keep the sauce warm.

To serve, turn out the terrine on to a warmed dish and slice it. Cover the slices with a little sauce and sprinkle them with the remaining tablespoon of chopped chives. Hand the remaining sauce separately. HM

MUSSELS 'LA PRÉE'

'La Prée' is a seaside restaurant near the small port of Pornic, near Brittany, where this recipe originates. Although mussels can be kept in the refrigerator for 1–2 days, it is best to cook them on the day of purchase. Scraping and cleaning the mussels should be done as close to the cooking time as possible.

SERVES 6 AS A SUPPER DISH, OR 8 AS A FIRST COURSE

3kg/6lb 10oz mussels
50g/2oz butter
200g/7oz onions, finely chopped
2 garlic cloves, finely chopped
275ml/½ pint dry white wine
1 sprig fresh, or 1 teaspoon dried, thyme
1 bay leaf
½ teaspoon freshly ground black pepper
2 tablespoons chopped parsley
freshly ground black pepper
flaked sea salt

FOR THE HOLLANDAISE SAUCE
500g/1lb 2oz butter
6 egg yolks
juice of 2 lemons

To make the Hollandaise sauce, start by clarifying the butter. Melt the butter on a low heat, then let it stand for at least 5 minutes until all the butter oil has risen to the top. Remove any butter impurities, skim off all the butter oil, and discard any watery buttermilk that has settled in the bottom of pan. Keep the clarified butter warm.

Combine the egg yolks and lemon juice in a heavy-bottomed pan and whisk the mixture to a foam, preferably using a balloon whisk. Place the pan over a low heat and continue to whisk until the egg foam begins to thicken, and then remove from the heat. Whisk in the warm butter, a tablespoon at a time, until the butter and foam start to emulsify, then whisk in the rest of the butter in a slow steady stream. It should be a thick sauce.

Season with salt and pepper to taste, and keep the sauce warm, but not hot, while you cook the mussels.

Clean the mussels, scraping any barnacles off the shells using the back of a small knife, and pull off the 'beards'. Rinse in lots of cold water and discard any open mussels or those with cracked or broken shells.

Heat the butter in a large pan over a medium heat. Add the onions and garlic and cook for 1–2 minutes, stirring occasionally. Add the wine, thyme, bay leaf and pepper, stir well and bring to the boil. Tip in the mussels and cover with a lid or foil and cook on a high heat for 6–7 minutes or until the mussels are just open. Halfway through cooking shake the pan and turn the mussels over with a slotted spoon to ensure even cooking.

Take off the heat, and discard any mussels that have not opened. Strain the cooking juices through a sieve lined with a moist muslin cloth, and whisk 3 tablespoons of the juice into the sauce.

When the mussels are cool enough to handle, remove and discard one shell from each mussel. Arrange the mussels in a large ovenproof dish, pour over the Hollandaise sauce and sprinkle with the chopped parsley. **HM**

ONCE-A-YEAR BOLTON ABBEY OYSTERS

A friend of over forty years, who was at school with our son Sto (Hartington), comes to stay with us at Bolton Abbey every August. He lives in furthest Argyll and has an oyster bed. This generous man brings enough of his harvest to feed a lot of people at dinner. There is a kitchen pantomime of landlubbers trying to open them, which ends with the oysterman himself busy with this task after his long drive. The oysters have become a tradition, one of the excitements of Bolton. **DD**

Although this is a complicated dish, almost all of it can be made a day in advance, and the last-minute work is quick and easy.

SERVES 6

36 large fresh oysters

rock salt for bedding

flaked sea salt

freshly ground black pepper

FOR THE FILLING

75g/3oz good beef dripping or butter

1 medium onion, finely diced

1 celery stick, finely diced

3 garlic cloves, finely chopped

55ml/2fl oz Ricard or Pernod

juice of 1 lemon

a few shakes of Tabasco sauce

2 tablespoons Worcestershire sauce

750g/1lb 10oz spinach leaves

6 anchovy fillets in oil, puréed

75g/3oz fresh white breadcrumbs

FISH SAUCE FOR COATING OYSTERS

50g/2oz butter

25g/1oz flour

½ medium onion, peeled and
   chopped finely

150ml/¼ pint white wine

275ml/½ pint fish stock (see page 29)

150ml/¼ pint double cream

3 egg yolks

1 tablespoon Ricard or Pernod

Rinse the oysters in cold water. Open one by holding it firmly in a folded kitchen cloth (to protect your hand), with the flatter shell on top and with the pointed hinged end facing you. Insert the blade of an oyster knife between the shells at the hinge and prise them open. Now slide the knife along the top (flat) shell to cut the small muscle that links the two shells. Discard the top shell. Strain the oyster juices into a bowl through a fine mesh, scoop the oyster out into a pan and reserve the rounded, bottom shell. Repeat the process until you have opened all the oysters.

Pour the strained juices over the oysters and bring to the boil for just one second and then immediately remove from the heat. Leave the oysters to cool in their cooking liquor and then refrigerate.

Rinse the rounded shells in hot water (but no detergent), dry them and set aside.

Now make the filling. Drain the liquor from the cooked mussels. Cook the spinach, drain it and refresh under cold running water, and chop it coarsely. Set aside. Melt the beef dripping or butter in a pan over a moderate heat, add the onion and celery and fry for a few minutes, before adding the garlic. Continue to cook until all the vegetables are soft. Then add the Ricard or Pernod, the liquor from the cooked oysters, the lemon juice and the Tabasco and Worcestershire sauces, and bring these to the boil. Add the spinach and anchovy purée, and bring the mixture rapidly and briefly back to the boil before removing it from the heat. Spoon the mixture into a food processor and blend it briefly. Add enough breadcrumbs to soak up juices – the mixture should be firm – and season to taste. Cool and refrigerate.

Spread rock salt to a depth of about 1cm/½in in ovenproof serving dishes. This will support the filled oysters.

Spoon a walnut-sized dollop of filling into each shell, top with an oyster and then spread a thin layer of filling over each oyster (just enough to keep the oysters moist when they are reheated in the oven). Cover with foil and refrigerate.

Start to make the fish sauce by melting 25g/1oz of the butter over a moderate heat, adding the flour, and cooking for a few minutes, stirring from time to time, until the roux is a pale golden colour. Set aside. Melt the remaining butter over a moderate heat, add the onion and cook until it is soft, without letting it colour. Pour in the wine, bring it to the boil to reduce the acidity, then add the fish stock and return to the boil. Now thicken the mixture by incorporating the cooled roux, whisking continuously to make a smooth sauce of coating consistency. Simmer for a few minutes before taking the sauce off the heat and setting it aside. (At this stage you could let it cool and refrigerate for a day.)

Half an hour before serving, preheat the oven to 200C/400F/Gas 6.

Take the oysters out of the fridge and put them in the oven, still covered with foil, to reheat for about 15 minutes.

Meanwhile, reheat the sauce and whip the cream until it forms soft peaks. Whisk the egg yolks into the warm sauce, add the Ricard or Pernod and whisk in the cream. Season to taste, spoon over the warmed oysters, and serve immediately. **HM**

POULTRY
& GAME

E ACH MAN KILLS the thing he loves, but he doesn't necessarily eat it. Never mind, we eat lots of chicken here as, luckily, the cooked birds are anonymous so sentiment doesn't come into it. Chicken is now the universal mass-produced food we know so well and see everywhere. C heap, versatile, rarely offending, it turns up in any number of guises and disguises, some more welcome than others. Time was when chicken was an expensive treat, and the age, breeding and feeding were taken into account by sellers and buyers. Perhaps we are beginning to see the return of that interest, but I still can't find either the breed or the exact method of feeding of the wonderful Poulet de Bresse so often on the menu in French restaurants. No chicken in this country is quite like it. The table birds in the Farm Shop are Rosses and Cobbs, specially bred for that purpose and killed at 8–10 weeks old. Their ancestors were the old 'heavy' breeds of poultry, which matured much more slowly than these hybrids and would therefore cost too much to rear now, when a speedy turnover is everything.

If you live in the country you are aware of game and all it means – both to the local economy and, now, politically. The sport it provides is the source of great enjoyment for those who take part in it, as well as giving us a variety of unusual food. The seasonal pleasures, in the hunting as well as in the eating, start on 12th August when grouse appear on the table while the northern summer still pretends to rule. According to the *Encyclopaedia Britannica*, *Lagopus scoticus*, unique to these islands, was the cause of 'events of some importance in the annals of North Britain which followed from its pursuit in Caithness in 1157'. What events? Is there a student of twelfth-century Scotch history who can tell us? And the Glorious Twelfth is said to have decided the date of the Parliamentary summer recess.

I wonder if this influential bird would still be the reason for people to book tables at the best restaurants to eat the first grouse of the season if the customers knew that each is host to an average of two thousand worms. 'Hopefully only one thousand,' the Bolton Abbey keeper tells me, 'three and a half thousand is getting towards fatal in old birds.' The charm of grouse is that they really are wild birds. No attempt at rearing them artificially succeeds as it does with partridges and pheasants. They are dependent on a staple diet of young heather shoots, the weather – a thundery downpour in late May can drown the young chicks – and being undisturbed at nesting time. And these ground-nesting birds are prey to all the predators known to gamekeepers.

Partridges are in season from September. Cook them like grouse and they are surely the best game bird to eat. They are a rare example in food of English being better than French. The former, grey partridges, are compact and plump, whereas the French variety do too much running on their red legs and are lean and stringy and hardly worth cooking.

After partridges comes the hunter's moon with short days, frosts and other hardships. This is the time for pheasants, which are cheap when they are in season and need not be dull at all. **DD**

STEAMED STUFFED CHICKEN BREAST WITH MUSHROOM AND PORT SAUCE, AND SAVOURY RICE

Steaming chicken used to be the way with old birds, the slow cooking getting rid of any toughness in the meat. The receipt is better still if a chicken in its prime is used. DD

SERVES 6

50g/2oz butter

350g/12oz leeks, cleaned and cut into 5cm/2in strips

1 tablespoon chopped fresh tarragon

6 x 175g/6oz free range chicken breasts, boned and skinned

flaked sea salt

freshly ground black pepper

1 tablespoon chopped parsley

FOR THE MUSHROOM AND PORT SAUCE

1.2l/2 pints white chicken stock (see page 27)

25g/1oz butter

50g/2oz shallots, finely chopped

2 cloves garlic, finely chopped

1 bay leaf

1 sprig fresh thyme

200ml/7fl oz port

400g/14oz white mushrooms, cut in half and finely sliced

275ml/½ pint double cream

FOR THE SAVOURY RICE

570ml/1 pint white chicken stock

75g/3oz butter

300g/11oz onion, finely chopped

2 cloves garlic, finely chopped

1 bay leaf

2 sprigs fresh, or 1 teaspoon dried, thyme

175g/6oz chicken livers, cleaned (see top of page 71), and cut into 5mm/¼in dice

300g/11oz long grain rice

Start by making the leek filling for the chicken. Melt the butter in a pan over a low heat, add the leeks and tarragon and cook until they are soft. Season to taste and set aside to cool.

Slice horizontally two-thirds of the way through each chicken breast, and open them out, keeping each in one piece. Lightly dampen the breasts with cold water. Cover with clingfilm and, using a rolling pin, bat each one out to a thickness of about 1cm/½in. Season on both sides. Divide the leeks evenly among the chicken breasts and roll the chicken into sausage shapes, ensuring the leeks stay in the centre. Wrap each roll in clingfilm and tie both ends with string, so they look like Christmas crackers. Refrigerate until you are ready to steam them. (The rolls can be refrigerated overnight at this stage.)

To make the sauce, start by reducing the stock to a syrup by boiling it steadily until there is about 275ml/½ pint left. Meanwhile melt the butter in a pan over a medium heat, add the shallots and garlic and cook for a few minutes until they soften. Pour in the port, add the bay leaf and thyme, and boil to reduce the liquid by half. Add the mushrooms and cook for 2–3 minutes. Pour in the cream, add the chicken syrup and boil again to reduce the mixture until it is thick enough to coat the back of a spoon. Remove the herbs and check the seasoning. Take off the heat, cover and set aside. (At this stage the sauce can be cooled and refrigerated overnight.)

When you are ready to cook the chicken, set water to boil in a steamer and preheat the oven to 180C/350F/Gas 4 for the rice. (The rice and chicken should be ready at the same time.)

Put the chicken to steam for 20 minutes.

To cook the rice, heat up the chicken stock to boiling point. In another pan, melt the butter over medium heat, add the onions and garlic and cook until they soften. Add the bay leaf and thyme. Turn up the heat and cook the diced chicken livers for 2–3 minutes. Add the rice and pour in the boiling chicken stock. Bring back to the boil, and then transfer the contents of the pan into an ovenproof dish. Cover tightly or seal with foil and bake in the oven for 15–20 minutes.

Lift the chicken out of the steamer and remove the clingfilm, pouring any juices into the sauce. Reheat the sauce gently.

To serve, slice the chicken breast rolls into 4 or 5 even slices, keeping them together to retain the sausage shape. Lift gently on to a warmed serving dish, pour over the hot sauce and sprinkle with the parsley. Hand the rice separately. TTM

GRILLED CHICKEN
WITH CHICORY AND AUBERGINE
AND RED WINE SAUCE

SERVES 6

6 x 200g/7oz chicory spears

juice of 1 lemon

1 teaspoon caster sugar

4 x 225g/8oz aubergines, peeled,
   topped and tailed, cut into
   2.5cm/1in slices

110g/4oz butter

6 x 225g/8oz boneless free range
   chicken breasts with the skin on

25g/1oz clarified butter

200ml/7fl oz olive oil

flaked sea salt

freshly ground black pepper

1 tablespoon finely chopped parsley

FOR THE RED WINE SAUCE

50g/2oz shallots, finely sliced

2 garlic cloves, finely sliced

1 tablespoon cider vinegar

½ tablespoon caster sugar

1 bay leaf

1 sprig fresh, or ½ teaspoon dried,
   thyme

200ml/7fl oz red wine

½ tablespoon lightly crushed black
   peppercorns

1 rasher of smoked bacon, diced

275ml/½ pint brown chicken stock
   (see page 28)

Cook the chicory spears several hours in advance, because they need to drain well. Put them in a large sauté pan with 100ml/3½fl oz of water, the lemon juice and sugar and season with 1 tablespoon flaked sea salt and ½ teaspoon freshly ground black pepper. Bring to the boil, cover, turn down the heat and simmer for about 30 minutes or until tender. Transfer to a cooling rack to drain.

An hour or so before you are ready to start cooking the chicken, sprinkle the aubergine slices with a little sea salt on both sides. Leave them to stand until pearls of moisture come to the surface – this will draw out some of the bitterness.

Meanwhile, make the red wine sauce. Place all the ingredients except the stock in a medium-sized pan and cover with the wine. Bring to the boil and continue to boil over a moderate heat until almost all the liquid has evaporated. Add the stock. Bring to the boil and reduce until the sauce reaches a light coating consistency. Check the seasoning. Strain through a fine sieve into a small saucepan. Cover and keep warm.

Melt the butter in a large frying pan over a moderate heat. When it begins to turn brown add the drained chicory spears and cook them until they are brown them all over and slightly caramelised. This will take about 15 minutes. Season with salt and pepper. Set aside and keep warm.

Preheat the oven to 180C/350F/Gas 4, and heat up a ridged griddle pan over a moderate heat.

Season the chicken breasts and smear them with the clarified butter. Cook them skin-side down on the griddle pan for about 10 minutes, then turn them over and cook for a further 10 minutes. Make sure they are thoroughly cooked before transferring them to a dish to rest and keep warm.

Wipe the aubergine slices dry with kitchen paper. Heat the oil over a moderate heat and fry the slices on both sides until they are browned. Transfer to an ovenproof dish and bake in the oven for about 15–20 minutes until they are soft. Set aside and keep warm.

To serve, cut the chicken breasts into 2cm/¾in slices. Cut each chicory spear in half lengthways. Arrange alternating slices of aubergine, chicken and chicory on a hot ovenproof dish. Return to the oven for 3–4 minutes to make sure everything is hot, and then pour over all the red wine sauce and sprinkle with the chopped parsley. **HM**

STIR-FRIED GUINEA FOWL IN GARLIC AND WHISKY WITH STIR-FRIED VEGETABLES

This is particularly good served on a bed of mashed potatoes.

SERVES 4

4 guinea fowl breasts, skinless

flour for dusting

6 tablespoons vegetable oil

2 shallots, finely chopped

2 garlic cloves, finely chopped

100g/4oz butter

25g/1oz chopped parsley

3 tablespoons whisky

a pinch of sugar

3 tablespoons soy sauce

150ml/¼ pint brown chicken stock (see page 28)

flaked sea salt

freshly ground black pepper

BATCH 1 VEGETABLES

50g/2oz celery, cut into 3cm/1¼in strips

50g/2oz red onion, finely sliced

50g/2oz carrot, cut into 3cm/1¼in strips

50g/2oz blanched shredded cabbage, parboiled for a few minutes, refreshed and drained

25g/1oz grated fresh ginger

50g/2oz leek, cut into 3cm/1¼in strips

BATCH 2 VEGETABLES

50g/2oz cucumber, peel on, cut into 3cm/1¼in strips

50g/2oz courgette, peel on, cut into 3cm/1¼in strips

50g/2oz mushrooms, sliced

Prepare the vegetables, keeping Batches 1 and 2 separate. Using a wok or frying pan over a high heat, stir-fry the Batch 1 vegetables in 2 tablespoons of hot oil, until they are al dente (wilted but firm). Tip on to a warm serving dish and keep hot. Repeat the process with Batch 2, then mix the vegetables together.

Cut each guinea fowl breast into 5 slices. Season the slices with salt and pepper and dust with the flour. Heat the remaining 2 tablespoons of oil in the same wok or frying pan, add the shallots and the guinea fowl and stir-fry over a high heat for about 5–8 minutes until the meat is cooked. Arrange the meat over the vegetables.

Mix the garlic, butter and chopped parsley together. Put these in the wok or frying pan, and add the whisky, sugar, soy sauce and brown chicken stock. Stir until everything is hot.

Pour the sauce over the meat and vegetables and serve immediately. **AB**

DERBYSHIRE STUFFING

This lemon, thyme and parsley stuffing, known at Chatsworth as Derbyshire Stuffing, is particularly good with roast chicken. Although it can be put into the breast end of the bird before roasting, we usually cook it separately, as described below.

MAKES 8 X 50G/2OZ BALLS
OR ENOUGH TO STUFF 2 CHICKENS

50g/2oz butter
100g/4oz onion, finely diced
3 tablespoons chopped fresh, or 1
   tablespoon dried, thyme
3 tablespoons chopped parsley
grated zest and juice of 1 unwaxed
   lemon

50g/2oz fresh white or brown
   breadcrumbs
225g/8oz best pork sausage meat
   (preferably 100 per cent pork)
1 egg, beaten

Preheat the oven to 220C/425F/Gas 7.

Melt the butter in a pan over a low heat, add the onion and cook for 10 minutes until it is soft but not coloured. Set aside to cool. Combine the herbs, lemon zest and breadcrumbs in a bowl, then add the cooled onions, sausage meat, lemon juice and egg, and mix thoroughly. Either stuff the birds, or roll the mixture into 3 4cm/1½in balls and place on a buttered baking sheet. Bake in the oven for about 30 minutes. **AB**

ROAST PHEASANT OR GROUSE
WITH TRIMMINGS

There is a tradition at Chatsworth of serving roast pheasant or grouse with several different trimmings. Of these, the corn pudding, the bread sauce, the fried crumbs and the apples and chestnuts can be made in advance and reheated. One of the specialities of the house is the parsnip crisps, but you do need a deep fryer to make these. Using a deep fryer is also by far the best way to cook and peel the chestnuts, although you can buy ready-peeled, vacuum-packed chestnuts. We recycle many of the left-overs: we serve the corn pudding cold with meat and salads; we use the bread sauce to make horseradish sauce by adding cream, freshly grated horseradish and English mustard, and the fried crumbs and parsnip crisps are used as toppings for green salads. The birds' carcasses are made into brown stock and the meat is either served cold, devilled (see page 112), or used in game soup.

SERVES 6

3 x 750g/1lb 10oz hen pheasants
    (with wish-bones removed for ease
    of carving) or 6 x 350g/12oz grouse
110g/4oz clarified butter
110ml/4fl oz red wine
570ml/1 pint brown chicken stock
    (see page 28) or game stock
flaked sea salt
freshly ground black pepper

FOR THE CORN PUDDING
25g/1oz butter for greasing
1 x 326g tin of sweetcorn
2 free range eggs
1 egg yolk
200ml/7fl oz double cream
200ml/7fl oz milk
1 tablespoon plain flour
2 tablespoons chopped chives
⅔ teaspoon grated nutmeg

FOR THE FRIED CRUMBS
150g/5oz clarified butter
150g/5oz fresh white breadcrumbs
a pinch of salt

FOR THE BREAD SAUCE
50g/2oz butter
150g/5oz onions, finely chopped
570ml/1 pint milk
150ml/¼ pint double cream
3 bay leaves
1 teaspoon black peppercorns
2 cloves
125g/4½oz fresh white breadcrumbs
⅓ teaspoon grated nutmeg

FOR THE SAUTÉED APPLES
WITH CHESTNUTS
400g/14oz fresh chestnuts, or
    250g/8oz vacuum-packed peeled
    chestnuts
100g/4oz butter
6 eating apples (Cox, Granny Smith)
    peeled, cored and cut into quarters
a pinch of sugar
50ml/2fl oz Calvados
1 tablespoon chopped parsley

FOR THE PARSNIP CRISPS
450g/1lb parsnips, peeled and washed

TO MAKE THE CORN PUDDING: preheat the oven to 180C/350F/Gas 4, and
butter a one-pint (15cm/6in diameter) soufflé dish. Drain the sweetcorn
and squeeze dry. Finely chop, or process, half the sweetcorn. Whisk
together the eggs, the egg yolk, cream, milk, flour, chopped chives, and
nutmeg, and season with salt and pepper. Add the sweetcorn purée and
kernels and pour the mixture into the soufflé dish. Stand the dish in a deep

roasting tin and pour in enough boiling water to come halfway up the dish. Cook in the oven for about 1½ hours until set. Leave to stand, but keep warm.

TO MAKE THE PARSNIP CRISPS: preheat a deep fryer to 180C/350F. Slice the parsnips as thinly as possible (ideally to the thickness of a 1p coin). Deep fry a small amount at a time until crisp and golden. Drain and sprinkle with salt and coarsely ground black pepper.

TO MAKE THE BREAD SAUCE: melt 25g/1oz of the butter in a heavy saucepan over a moderate heat and cook the onions for about 5 minutes to soften them, but don't let them colour. Add the milk, cream, bay leaves, peppercorns and cloves, and bring to the boil. Remove from the heat and set aside for about half an hour to let the flavours infuse. Strain, then bring the milk and cream to the boil again. Stir in the breadcrumbs to thicken, and then add the grated nutmeg and the remaining butter. Cover with clingfilm and keep warm.

TO MAKE THE FRIED CRUMBS: melt the clarified butter in a pan over a moderate heat, add the breadcrumbs and stir until golden. Add a pinch of salt and set aside.

TO MAKE THE SAUTÉED APPLES WITH CHESTNUTS: if you are using fresh chestnuts, top and tail them so you can just see the flesh; then deep fry them at 180C/350F for 3 minutes. Cover with a cloth and leave them to stand for a few minutes. Using a small knife, remove the shells and brown skins.

In a frying pan large enough to hold the apples and chestnuts, heat the butter (or, if you have any, chicken or game fat) over a medium heat. Sauté the apple quarters until golden. Add the sugar, pour on the Calvados and then add the chestnuts. Cook for a few minutes, drain off any fat, sprinkle with the chopped parsley and set aside.

TO ROAST THE BIRDS: preheat the oven to 180C/350F/Gas 4. Smear each bird with clarified butter and season with salt and pepper inside and out. Place the birds on their backs in a roasting tin, leaving a gap of 5cm/2in between each. Roast pheasant for about 35 minutes and grouse for 20 minutes, basting them regularly. Remove from the oven and set aside to rest in a warm place for at least 30 minutes.

Set the roasting tin over a gentle heat and allow the juices and sediments to settle and colour without burning. Drain off the fat, reserving it for future use. Add the red wine and brown stock to the juices in the tray and simmer for a few minutes. Correct the seasoning and pass the gravy through a fine strainer into a pan.

TO SERVE: first cut the wings off the birds and then cut off the legs. For pheasants, carve each breast into 4 slices lengthways; for grouse, cut each bird in half and remove the breast bone. Place the breast meat in the centre of a warm serving dish, surround it with apple and chestnut garnish, and then arrange the legs on the outside rim of the dish. Drizzle a little gravy over the breasts. Hand the rest of the gravy, the bread sauce, the fried crumbs, corn pudding and parsnip crisps separately HM

DEVILLED PHEASANT

This is the time-honoured way of using left-over cooked pheasant. We usually serve it accompanied by plain boiled rice.

SERVES 6

25g/1oz butter, plus extra for greasing

1½ tablespoons plain flour

½ teaspoon English mustard powder

275ml/½ pint milk

150ml/¼ pint double cream

½ teaspoon flaked sea salt

a pinch of cayenne pepper

1½ tablespoons Worcestershire sauce

½ tablespoon mushroom ketchup

a dash of Tabasco sauce

1 cooked pheasant, or 300g/10oz cooked pheasant meat

Preheat the oven to 200C/400F/Gas 6.

Melt the butter in a pan over a medium heat and whisk in the flour and mustard. Cook for about a minute, whisking regularly. Heat the milk and cream to almost boiling point and pour them into the roux, whisking continuously. Add the salt, cayenne pepper, Worcestershire sauce, mushroom ketchup and Tabasco sauce and simmer for 10 minutes. Meanwhile, take all the meat off the pheasant and/or shred roughly with your hands. Put it in a greased ovenproof dish and pour the sauce over it. Bake in the oven for 10 minutes, until the top is nicely browned. **DW**

LAMB,
PORK &
BEEF

I FEEL SORRY FOR VEGETARIANS because they miss so much. Think of no more gravy, imagine no Irish stew or oxtail or ham. Now that we never see it, I sometimes dream of the forgotten treat of beef dripping on toast and digging for the brown bits at the bottom. If they were forbidden, bacon, tongue, steak and kidney pudding, cutlets and the indescribably delicious Scotch collops would soon become an obsession.

Conversely, nasty meat, tough and dry, puts you off the whole subject and I am amazed by people who buy expensive bright red fillet steak with no hint of fat round it in the hope that the price will guarantee something good. It doesn't.

I asked Paul Neale, the head butcher in our Farm Shop, why our meat has such a good reputation. 'We guarantee proper hanging of beef and venison, and our customers appreciate the difference. Our beef hangs for a minimum of ten to fourteen days in carcass, then it is butchered and not sold for another week – making nearly three weeks in all. Wild boar is hung for seven days and venison for ten days.'

What the supermarket customer cannot judge is how long the beef has been hung. It is vital to the 'eating quality' of beef that it should hang for a minimum of two weeks. During this time the meat shrinks and takes on a darker colour. Paul told me 'It starts at the edge and the meat is mature when it is half an inch dark all over. You never see a piece of meat with a dark edge in a supermarket. It would be removed because it would not look as attractive as an overall impression of bright red enhanced by lighting.' As beef is sold by weight, it is the shrinking (and of course the valuable space it takes up while hanging) that the big shops don't like. Theirs is cut up as soon as it is killed – hence the bright colour. This speedy treatment produces a meat that is quite different from that hung in the old-fashioned way and it is no wonder that the former is becoming less popular.

Paul tells me that his customers usually ask for 'a nice piece of lean meat'. They will not buy it with the fat in it, but when offered a separate slice of fat to help the cooking they rarely refuse, which only goes to show there's nowt so queer as folks.

People who come to the Farm Shop can see the cows and their suckled calves, as well as ewes and lambs, grazing in the fields that surround it and it gives them confidence that the creatures are decently reared in their natural surroundings. The other thing which appeals to our customers is the real live butcher in the shop who will cut what you want and how you want it. The display on the meat counter is a work of art and packs of different cuts of lamb and beef fly out of the shop. The farmer and the butcher learn what is wanted by the customer and the

André Birkett behind the meat counter at the Farm Shop.
Paul Neale is working at the chopping block.

customer learns too. Soon after the Farm Shop opened a woman who bought a whole lamb pack wrote to me in disgust. 'When I drive through the park I see the lambs and they have four legs, so why are there only two in the pack I bought?' She had never heard of a shoulder of lamb.

Since the BSE scare, brains have been banned. My father would have been dismayed by this rule and I expect he would have furiously disregarded it. When Mark Ogilvie-Grant, a fastidious and effeminate friend of twenty-year-old Nancy, bravely came to stay with us and unwillingly obeyed orders to arrive in the dining room at 8 a.m., my father greeted the poor fellow with, 'Brains for breakfast, Mark. Pig's thinkers – can't beat 'em.'

Thinkers are out, but rare breeds are in. Our butchery is accredited in the Rare Breeds Survival Trust Traditional Breeds Meat Marketing Scheme and, when they are available, we sell Gloucester Old Spot, Middle White and Tamworth pigs, and British White, White Park and Dexter cattle. Each of these has their own fans. The Devonshires have kept Jacob sheep since 1839. We have a flock of fifty of these four-horned, piebald characters straight out of the Bible, whose wool must have provided Jacob's coat of many colours. Not long ago they were a rare breed, but they are popular now for their attractive appearance and slightly gamey meat. Five thousand more ewes, Mashams and the curiously named Mules, graze the park and its surrounding fields, and Speckled Faced Swaledales run on the moor. The rams we use are Suffolk, Texel and Rouge de l'Ouest. Even the Farm Shop can't take all the harvest of lambs. The surplus are sold at our own sheep sale, held on the farm in September. It is said to be the biggest one-day sale from a single owner in the country. DD

IRISH STEW

There are dozens of receipts for Irish stew, but this simple one is our favourite.
The barley is vital; so are the dumplings. DD

SERVES 6

1.3kg/3lb neck of lamb, meat and
  bones (ask your butcher to remove
  the bones – but make sure you keep
  the bones for the stock – and to
  remove the elastine from the meat)
½ onion, sliced
75g/3oz pearl barley
1 garlic clove, finely chopped
1 tablespoon chopped fresh rosemary
1 tablespoon chopped fresh thyme
18 new potatoes
18 pickling onions
flaked sea salt
freshly ground black pepper

FOR THE STOCK
the bones from the neck of lamb
1 onion, roughly chopped
1 carrot, roughly chopped
2 celery sticks, roughly chopped
1 garlic clove
sprigs of thyme, parsley and a bay
  leaf (bouquet garni)
8 white peppercorns

FOR THE DUMPLINGS
110g/4oz self-raising flour
50g/2oz suet
1 tablespoon chopped parsley
1 tablespoon chopped chives
1 tablespoon chopped chervil

Make the stock by putting the bones in a pan with all the other stock ingredients and covering them with cold water. Bring to the boil, simmer gently for 1½ hours and then strain, reserving only the liquor.

Preheat the oven to 180C/350F/Gas 4.

Cut the meat into 5cm/2in pieces. Stir the meat with the sliced onion, pearl barley, garlic, rosemary, thyme, salt and pepper in a bowl. Put one-third of the meat mixture in a large casserole dish. Arrange 6 potatoes and 6 of the pickling onions on the meat. Repeat the layers until all the meat, potatoes and onions are used up. Pour in enough hot stock to cover all the ingredients, cover and cook in the oven for 1½–2 hours.

Make the dumplings by mixing the ingredients with 55ml/2fl oz of water to form a dough. Split this into 6 equal pieces and roll into balls. About 15 minutes before the end of the cooking time add the dumplings to the stew. The dumplings will double in size once they are cooked. **DW**

MINTED LOIN OF LAMB WITH WOODLAND SAUCE

The sauce can be made a day in advance, and the vegetables and topping can be prepared a few hours in advance. For 12 servings you will need two 6-boned racks of lamb (about 450g/1lb per person).

	NUMBER OF SERVINGS	
	12	24
carrots, chopped	3	6
onions, chopped	3	6
sticks of celery, chopped	3	6
leeks, washed and chopped	3	6
bay leaves	3	6
vegetable oil	4 tablespoons	6 tablespoons
6-bone rack of lamb	5kg/12lb	10kg/24lb
water	1l/1¾ pints	2l/3½ pints
flaked sea salt		
freshly ground black pepper		
FOR THE CRUMBLE TOPPING		
white breadcrumbs	300g/10oz	600g/1lb 4oz
chopped mint	50g/2oz	100g/4oz
butter, melted	120g/4oz	250g/8oz
FOR THE WOODLAND SAUCE		
dried wild mushrooms	120g/4oz	250g/8oz
warm water to soak mushrooms	150ml/¼ pint	300ml/½ pint

truffle oil	4 tablespoons	150ml/¼ pint
onions, finely chopped	250g/8oz	500g/1lb
garlic cloves, crushed	1	2
red wine	350ml/12fl oz	700ml/24fl oz
bay leaves	2	4
vegetable stock	1.2l/2 pints	2.4l/4 pints
beurre manié (equal parts of soft butter and flour mixed to a paste)	60g/2oz	120g/4oz
tomatoes, skinned, deseeded and diced	60g/2oz	120g/4oz
pine nuts, toasted	60g/2oz	120g/4oz
parsley, chopped	10g/½oz	20g/1oz
chives, chopped	10g/½oz	20g/1oz

Start by soaking the mushrooms (for the sauce) in the water for 25 minutes.

Preheat the oven to 220C/425F/Gas 7. Place the chopped vegetables and the bay leaves in a roasting tin and season.

To cook the lamb, start by heating the oil in a frying pan over a medium heat and put in the meat, skin-side down. Once the skin is browned, turn it over to seal the underside for one minute and then seal each end of the meat for one minute. Transfer the meat, skin-side up, on to the vegetables. Season the skin well with salt and pepper. Pour the water around the vegetables. Roast in the oven: for 15 minutes for rare, 20 minutes for medium, 25 minutes for medium to well done, and 30 minutes for well done meat.

Mix all the crumble topping ingredients together and season with salt and pepper. Five minutes before the end of the cooking time, press them on to the fatty side of the meat to form a crust.

While the meat is cooking, make the sauce. Drain the mushrooms, but reserve the liquor. Heat the truffle oil in a pan over a low heat, add the onions and garlic and cook until soft but not coloured. Add the drained mushrooms and cook for a further 2 minutes. Add the red wine and bay leaves, turn up the heat and cook until the liquid is reduced by half. Add the vegetable stock and the mushroom liquor to the sauce, bring it back to the boil and reduce by about a third. Add the beurre manié slowly, allowing it to cook thoroughly, stirring all the time to make a smooth sauce. Check the seasoning, and add the tomatoes, toasted pine nuts, parsley and chives. Keep warm until needed.

When the meat is cooked, take it out of the oven, lift it on to a warm dish and let it rest for 10 minutes before carving. Discard the vegetables and pan juices.

While the meat is resting, reheat the sauce. Serve the sauce poured over the carved meat. **PG**

NOISETTES OF LAMB
WITH PEA MOUSSE AND MADEIRA SAUCE

This dish can be prepared a day ahead, leaving you with only the sauce to reheat and the lamb to be cooked for 10–12 minutes just before serving.

SERVES 6

12 noisettes of lamb, each weighing
  about 75g/3oz (these will come from
  loins of lamb; ask your butcher to
  give you the bones for the sauce)
110ml/4fl oz vegetable oil
12 sheets of filo pastry, each about
  30 x 30cm/12 x 12in
4 egg yolks
flaked sea salt
freshly ground black pepper

FOR THE MADEIRA SAUCE
900g/2lb lamb bones
1 carrot, cut in half
1 onion, cut into four
1 leek, washed and roughly chopped

2 sticks celery, roughly chopped
2 garlic cloves, crushed
sprigs of thyme, parsley and a bay
  leaf (bouquet garni)
570ml/1 pint chicken stock (see
  page 27)
200ml/7fl oz Madeira

FOR THE PEA MOUSSE
25g/1oz butter
2 shallots, finely diced
2 garlic cloves, finely diced
350g/12oz peas or petit pois (fresh
  or frozen)
75ml/3fl oz cream
3 egg yolks, beaten

Preheat the oven to 230C/450F/Gas 8. To make the sauce, start by browning the bones: put them in a roasting tin and cook for about one hour or until they are browned all over. Transfer the bones to a large pan and add all the vegetables, including the garlic. De-glaze the roasting pan with 275ml/½ pint of water, scraping up all the sediments, and add this to the pan. Pour in the chicken stock and add the herbs. Bring to the boil, skim, and simmer for 1½ hours. Strain the stock, remove the bones and vegetables and discard them. Add the Madeira, bring to the boil again and reduce to a syrupy consistency. Check the seasoning and set aside.

Prepare the noisettes by seasoning them with salt and pepper. Heat the oil in a frying pan and seal the noisettes by frying them for a minute or two on each side. Leave them to cool on a rack, and then remove any string.

To make the the pea mousse, start by melting the butter over a medium heat and cooking the shallots and garlic for a few minutes. Add the peas or petit pois and 75ml/3fl oz of water, and cook until all the liquid has evaporated. Put the mixture into a food processor and blend to a purée. Add the cream and egg yolks, season with salt and pepper, and blend briefly again until the mixture is the texture of thick cream. Set aside.

Start to make filo pastry containers for the mousse by brushing one sheet of pastry with a thin layer of egg yolk (you may find this easier if you add a little water to the yolks). Place another sheet on top of the first and again brush with the yolks, and repeat with a third sheet. Treating the three sheets as one, cut the filo into 4 or 5 strips – each will be about 6 x 30cm/2½ x 12in. Repeat with the remaining filo sheets, until you have 12 strips.

Wrap a strip of filo pastry around the sides of each noisette so that the pastry forms a cylinder. The cylinders should stand up, forming filo pastry 'containers' about 3cm/1½in deep above each noisette. Put these into the fridge for 10 minutes so that the pastry dries out. (At this stage they can be left in the fridge overnight).

Half an hour before you want to serve the meat, preheat the oven to 220C/425F/Gas 7. Spoon the pea mousse into the pastry containers (on top of the lamb), and bake in the oven for 10–12 minutes.

While the lamb is cooking, reheat the sauce. Pour the sauce on to a large warmed serving dish, place the noisettes on top and serve immediately. DW

PAILLARDES OF PORK VIENNOISE

Most of the preparation for this dish can be done a day ahead. The last-minute cooking, including making the sauce, only takes a few minutes. The classic 'Viennoise' includes grated hard-boiled eggs, but to make it simpler, you could leave them out.

SERVES 6

750g1/1lb 12oz lean pork loin
350ml/13fl oz clarified butter or
   vegetable oil
flaked sea salt
freshly ground black pepper

FOR CRUMBING
3 eggs, beaten
100ml/4fl oz vegetable oil
75g/3oz flour
450g/1lb fresh white breadcrumbs

FOR THE VIENNOISE GARNISH
6 marinated pitted black olives
12 anchovy fillets in oil
2 lemons
6 eggs, hard boiled and grated
   (optional)

FOR THE VIENNOISE SAUCE
250g/9oz butter
250g/9oz brown chicken stock (see
   page 28)
juice of 1 lemon
50g/2oz mini capers in vinegar, drained
1 tablespoon chopped parsley

Prepare the garnish by cutting the pitted olives in half lengthways and rolling an anchovy fillet round each half. Cut each lemon into 6 equal wedges and set aside with the olives.

Prepare the meat by cutting it into 12 slices, each weighing about 60g/2½oz. Moisten each slice with a little cold water, place in a strong polythene freezer bag and, using a rolling pin, flatten to about 3mm/⅛in thick. Season these paillardes on both sides and set aside.

To crumb thte paillades, whisk the beaten eggs with the oil and season well. Spread the flour on one tray and the breadcrumbs on another. Coat each paillarde with flour, shake off any excess, then dip each in the egg mixture and then in the crumbs, coating evenly on both sides. Using a palette knife, gently press the coating to make sure it sticks firmly to the meat. If you want to store the paillardes in the fridge overnight, stack them with a layer of clingfilm or greaseproof paper between each.

Preheat the oven to 180C/350F/Gas 4.

Using a 30cm/12in frying pan, melt half the clarified butter or vegetable oil over a high heat. Add 3 of the paillardes and cook until they are golden brown on both sides. Then turn down the heat and fry for 2–3 more minutes, turning frequently until cooked. Place on a large serving dish and keep warm. Repeat the process. (You can strain the clarified butter and save it to use on another occasion.) Wipe the pan clean with kitchen paper, ready to make the sauce.

To make the sauce, melt the butter over a medium heat until lightly brown. Add the stock, lemon juice, capers and chopped parsley. Bring to a simmer for a minute or two. Season to taste.

To serve, sprinkle the paillardes with the grated hard-boiled eggs, if you are using them, pour the sauce over them and garnish with the olive and anchovy rolls and the lemon wedges. **HM**

LOIN OF PORK
WITH APPLE, BLACK PUDDING AND
CALVADOS ROLL

For every 12 servings, you will need three 4-boned loins of pork (about 160g/5–6oz per person). Ask your butcher to leave on a thin layer of fat, and to tie the loins. For every 12 servings, you will need the equivalent of a 30cm/13in puff pastry roll. These rolls can be prepared, but not cooked, a day ahead. The vegetables can be prepared a few hours ahead.

	NUMBER OF SERVINGS	
	12	24
carrots, chopped	3	6
onions, chopped	3	6
celery sticks, chopped	3	6
leeks, washed and chopped	3	6
bay leaves	3	6
vegetable oil	4 tablespoons	6 tablespoons
pork loins	2.4kg/5lb 4oz	4.8kg/10lb 8oz
water	1l/1¾ pints	2l/3½ pints
flaked sea salt		
freshly ground black pepper		

FOR THE PUFF PASTRY ROLL/S

chicken fillets, skinned	600g/1lb 4oz	1.2kg/2lb 8oz
egg whites	6	12
whipping cream	480ml/18fl oz	1l/1¾ pints
diced crispy bacon	300g/10oz	600g/1lb 4oz
Bramley apple, peeled and finely diced	450g/1lb	900g/2lb
Calvados	300ml/½ pint	600ml/1 pint
ready-made puff pastry	600g/1lb 4oz	1.2kg/2lb 8oz
eggs, beaten	6	12
black pudding	800g/1lb 12oz	1.6kg/3lb 8oz

Preheat the oven to 180C/350F/Gas 4.

Start by making the filling for the roll/s. Blend the chicken fillets in a food processor until they are smooth. Scrape the bowl, blend again and, with the motor running, slowly add the egg whites. Whip the cream to soft peaks, beat a quarter into the chicken mixture and then fold in the rest. Make sure it is well combined, and then fold in the bacon, apple and calvados. Season well with salt and pepper.

Roll out the pastry for the rolls on a well-floured surface: one rectangle of about 32 x 20cm/13 x 8in will make 12 servings. Ideally the pastry should be as thin as possible – about the thickness of a £1 coin. Divide the chicken mixture into equal quantities and spread in the centre of each pastry rectangle, leaving a 5cm/2in border. Brush the borders with the beaten egg.

Beat the black pudding to a piping consistency and, using a piping bag fitted with a plain 1cm/½in nozzle, pipe it along the centre of the chicken mixture on each rectangle.

Using both hands, wrap the pastry over the filling, sealing the edges with the beaten egg. Cut off any excess pastry at the short ends. Brush the roll/s well with beaten egg. Turn over so the seam is underneath, brush again and lift on to a greased baking sheet. Set aside until the meat is cooked. (At this stage the roll/s can be refrigerated overnight.)

Place the chopped vegetables and bay leaves in a roasting tin and season. Heat the oil in a pan and put in the meat, skin-side down. Once the skin is crisp and browned, turn the meat over to seal the underside for one minute and then seal each end of the meat for one minute. Transfer the meat, skin-side up, on to the vegetables. Season the skin well with salt and pepper. Pour the water around the vegetables and roast in the oven for 50 minutes. Remove from the oven, lift the meat on to a warm dish and let it rest for about 20 minutes before carving. Discard the vegetables, but reserve the pan juices to make gravy.

Turn up the oven to 190C/375F/Gas 5, and bake the roll/s for 25 minutes.

While the roll/s are cooking, make the gravy by reducing the pan juices to a syrupy consistency. Carve the meat and keep it warm. As soon as the roll/s are cooked, cut each into 12 slices and place on hot plates with the meat. Hand the gravy separately. **PG**

POT ROAST HAM WITH OATMEAL MUSTARD GLAZE AND MADEIRA GRAVY

This dish is served at Christmas and other festive occasions. Left-overs are served cold with Cumberland Sauce (page 191) or Careysville Spicy Oranges (page 192).

SERVES 15–20

5.4kg/12lb ham or gammon on the bone

110g/4oz pork dripping or clarified butter

8 garlic cloves

4 apples, peeled, cored and cut into quarters

3 sprigs fresh, or 1½ teaspoons dried, thyme

3 bay leaves

75g/3oz parsley

700g/1lb 8oz red onions, cut into 1cm/½in slices

350g/12oz carrots, cut on the slant into 1cm/½in slices

350g/12oz celery sticks, cut into 4cm/1½in pieces

450g/1lb button mushrooms

2 x 400g/14oz tins of chopped tomatoes in tomato juice

570ml/1pint Madeira

juice of 6 oranges

9 cloves

100g/4oz ready-made English mustard

1l/1¾ pints brown chicken stock (see page 28)

flaked sea salt

freshly ground black pepper

FOR THE GLAZE

110g/4oz pinhead oatmeal

225g/8oz light muscovado or demerara sugar

2 tablespoons English mustard powder

1½ teaspoons ground cloves

½ teaspoon ground cinnamon

1 tablespoon black peppercorns, lightly crushed

180ml/6fl oz Madeira

75g/3oz clear honey

Start a day in advance by leaving the ham or gammon to soak in cold water overnight to eliminate some of the salt. The next day, put it in a large pan and cover with fresh cold water. Bring to the boil, cover, and simmer for 40 minutes per kilo/15 minutes per pound. Allow to cool in the liquid for 3–4 hours.

When you are ready to cook, preheat the oven to 180C/350F/Gas 4.

Melt the dripping or clarified butter in a deep roasting tin that is large enough to hold the vegetables and the meat. Add the garlic, apples, herbs and all the vegetables, except the tomatoes. Cook over a medium heat for about 20 minutes, turning frequently, until they are golden brown. Take off the heat and add the tomatoes, Madeira and orange juice.

Lift the ham or gammon out of its cooking liquid. Cut off the rind and discard it, but leave on as much of the fat as possible. Score the fat into a diamond design and insert cloves in some of the crossing points. Place the ham on the vegetable mixture. Cover with foil and seal. Cook in the oven for 20 minutes per 500g/15 minutes per pound.

Prepare the glaze by mixing all the ingredients together in a bowl.

Half an hour before the end of its cooking time, take the meat out of the oven and discard the foil. Brush the fat with the ready-made mustard and then spread on the glaze using a palette knife. Heat the stock and pour it over the vegetables. Bake, uncovered, for a further 30 minutes, in order to allow the glaze to caramelise.

Remove the tin from the oven and set the meat aside to rest. Strain the vegetables over a saucepan to collect the juices. Place the vegetables towards one end of a large ovenproof serving dish, cover with foil and keep warm.

Allow the fat to settle on top of the juices, then skim it off. Bring the juices to the boil and reduce until they are the right syrupy consistency for a thin gravy. Check the seasoning and keep warm.

To serve, carve enough ham or gammon for the guests. Place the rest to the side of the vegetables, and lay the sliced meat over the vegetables, drizzling with the Madeira gravy. Hand the remaining gravy separately. HM

OXTAIL DAUBE WITH PARSNIP PURÉE

The oxtail is best if it is marinated for 48 hours, so start three days before you want to eat it. As well as adding flavour to the meat, the wine in the marinade helps to tenderise it.

SERVES 6

3 x 1kg/2lb 4oz oxtails (ask your butcher to joint them)

60g/2½oz plain flour, plus extra for coating the oxtail pieces

250ml/9fl oz vegetable oil

200ml/7fl oz port

4 medium tomatoes, quartered, or 1 x 400g/14oz tin of chopped tomatoes in tomato juice

250g/9oz smoked streaky bacon in one piece

2.25l/4 pints brown chicken stock (see page 28)

flaked sea salt

freshly ground black pepper

2 tablespoons chopped parsley

FOR THE MARINADE

2 x 750ml bottles of red wine

1 whole head of garlic, crushed

2 medium onions, cut into 2cm/¾in slices

2 large carrots, cut into 2cm/¾in rounds

4 celery sticks, cut into 2cm/¾in pieces

25g/1oz parsley, with stalks

2 sprigs fresh, or 1 teaspoon dried, thyme

2 bay leaves

40 black peppercorns, lightly crushed

75ml/3 fl oz olive oil

FOR THE PARSNIP PURÉE

500g/1lb parsnips, hard core removed, and cut into 2cm/¾in dice

250g/9oz potatoes, cut into 2cm/¾in dice

25g/1oz shallots, finely sliced

2 garlic cloves

570ml/1 pint milk

½ teaspoon grated nutmeg

75g/3oz butter

75ml/3fl oz olive oil

Prepare the marinade in a non-metallic container. Mix together all the ingredients except the olive oil. Stir in the meat, then pour over the olive oil. Seal with clingfilm and refrigerate for 48 hours.

When you are ready to cook, take the meat out of the marinade and leave it to drain in a colander. Strain the remaining marinade into a pan, reserving the vegetables. Bring the marinade to the boil, skim off any impurities, and boil until it is reduced by a third.

Preheat the oven to 160C/325F/Gas 3. Season the meat lightly with salt and pepper and coat it with flour, shaking off excess. Fry the meat in 3 batches in the vegetable oil in a heavy ovenproof pan over a high heat, browning it all over. Set aside. Turn down the heat a little, add the drained vegetables to the pan, and cook for about 5 minutes until they are golden brown.

Stir in 60g/2½oz of the flour and cook for 2–3 minutes. Pour in the marinade and port, and add the tomatoes, bacon and oxtail pieces. Cover with the stock, stir well and season with salt and pepper. Bring to the boil, cover, and cook in the oven for about 4 hours, stirring every 45 minutes or so, until the oxtails are tender and beginning to come away from the bone.

When the oxtails are cooked, lift them out of the pan with a slotted spoon and place on a shallow tray to cool. Strain the sauce into a large pan, using a fine mesh sieve, pressing down with a ladle to extract all the juices. Discard the vegetables, but keep the bacon (it can be diced into the sauce or eaten cold, or used as a garnish – on a quiche for example). Let the sauce settle, to allow the fat to rise to the surface (this will take about an hour), and skim off as much of the fat as you can. Bring the sauce to the boil and reduce to a syrupy, coating consistency, stirring from time to time.

In the meantime, trim any obvious gristle off the oxtail pieces and arrange the meat on an ovenproof serving dish. When the sauce is ready, check the seasoning, and pour it over the oxtail. Cover with foil and reheat in the oven for about 10 minutes.

Make the parsnip purée by placing the parsnips and potatoes in a pan with the shallots and garlic and a pinch of salt. Cover with the milk and 275ml/½ pint of water, bring to the boil and simmer over a moderate heat for about 20 minutes, until cooked. Drain, and either put the vegetables through a vegetable mill (mouli), or mash them thoroughly to make a purée. Add the nutmeg, butter and olive oil and season to taste.

Serve the oxtail sprinkled with the chopped parsley, and accompanied by the purée. **HM**

BRISKET OF BEEF WITH VEGETABLES AND A HERB DRESSING

The brisket instructions seem to go on for ever – making it is a real wet day's occupation. Even buying all the ingredients would take me half a day. But, never fear, the pleasure of eating it can last as long. The brisket can appear again and again: it is superb when cold and better each time for the keeping. I have included it because it is a classic that should not be forgotten. Its seldom-seen old-fashioned look and taste cannot be improved upon, so it is worth all the trouble in the end. DD

SERVES 10

2.5kg/5lb 8oz rolled brisket of beef
flaked sea salt
freshly ground black pepper

FOR THE BOUQUET GARNI
50g/2oz parsley, stalks on
3 sprigs fresh tarragon
2 sprigs fresh thyme
3 bay leaves
4 teaspoons black peppercorns, crushed
2 cloves
5 garlic cloves

FOR THE VEGETABLES
10 medium leeks, split open ⅔ of the
   way up, but root end left intact
1.1 kg/2lb 4oz swede, cut into 50g/2oz
   pieces
1.1 kg/2lb 4oz celeriac, cut into 50g/2oz
   pieces
900g/2lb celery, cut into 7.5cm/3in pieces
10 carrots, cut into 50g/2oz pieces

20 button onions
110ml/4fl oz white wine vinegar
20 x 40g/1½oz potatoes

FOR THE HERB DRESSING
55ml/2fl oz sherry vinegar
55ml/2fl oz balsamic vinegar
200ml/7fl oz walnut oil
200ml/7fl oz olive oil
1 level teaspoon flaked sea salt
½ teaspoon freshly ground pepper
75g/3oz shallots, finely chopped
50g/2oz capers, finely chopped
50g/2oz gherkins, finely chopped
2 tablespoons ready-made English
   mustard
1 garlic clove, finely chopped
6 anchovy fillets, finely diced
1 tablespoon chopped parsley
1 tablespoon chopped chives
1 tablespoon chopped tarragon

Prepare the brisket by soaking it in cold water for 2–3 hours to remove any excess brine. Make the bouquet garni by wrapping the ingredients in muslin and tying it up with string.

Half fill a large pan with 10l/17 pints of cold water and add the brisket. Bring to the boil and skim off any impurities that rise to the surface. Add the bouquet garni and simmer for 1½ hours.

Meanwhile prepare the vegetables. Wash the leeks thoroughly in cold water, and tie into a bundle with string. Top and tail the onions, leaving the roots intact. Bring about 1.2l/2 pints of water to the boil in a pan, and add the vinegar and then the onions. Take off the heat, cover and leave to stand for 15 minutes. Drain, discarding the water, and slip the skins off the onions. (This is a quick way to peel large quantities of onions; another advantage is that it avoids any tears.)

Make the herb dressing by mixing all the ingredients together in a bowl.

When the 1½ hours cooking time for the brisket is up, remove the bouquet garni and add all the vegetables, except the potatoes (because should any of the potatoes collapse during cooking, the stock will go cloudy). Bring it back to the boil. Simmer the brisket and vegetables for a further 45 minutes until the vegetables are tender. Taste, and add seasoning if required (the brisket adds salt to the water).

About 15 minutes after putting the vegetables in to cook, put the potatoes in a pan, cover them with some of the liquor from the brisket and simmer for 20 minutes or until cooked. Take off the heat, but leave the potatoes in the cooking liquor to keep warm.

To serve, take the vegetables and brisket out of the pan, and drain the potatoes. Remove the string from the leeks and put the leeks in the centre of a serving dish. Carve the meat into 5mm/¼in slices, across the grain, and arrange these on top of the leeks. Place the vegetables and potatoes around the meat and moisten with a little of the cooking liquor. Stir the dressing, drizzle a little over the meat, and hand the remaining dressing separately. **HM**

MY MOTHER'S SCOTCH COLLOPS

Mince? Well, sort of. It is certainly minced but is made of the best beef and tastes like it. Of all the receipts in this book, this is probably the easiest and quickest. A clue to its excellence is the name in Mrs Beeton: *'Beef Collops' (Escalope de Boeuf). The juice is like the beef tea of invalid days of childhood, irresistible when ill or well.* DD

SERVES 6

75g/3oz butter
675g/1lb 8oz beef fillet, freshly minced
2 tablespoons plain flour
150ml/¼ pint beef stock or water

3 slices of bread
flaked sea salt
freshly ground black pepper
1 tablespoon chopped parsley

Melt the butter in a large pan over a moderate heat, tip in the minced meat and stir until it is browned. Add the flour, mixing it well to soak up all the juices. Cook for 3–4 minutes and then add the stock or water. Season and cook for a further 5 minutes.

Meanwhile, toast the bread. Cut off the crusts and cut into 5mm/¼in dice.

Transfer the collops on to a hot dish, surround with the sippets of toast, sprinkle with the choped parsley, and serve piping hot. DW

VEGETABLES

&

SALAD

'THERE'S NO EXCUSE for coarsely mashed potatoes,' Eddie Sackville West declared to us, hugging his knees to his chest as he always did when moved. He had been to lunch with some neighbours in Co. Waterford who were strictly of the meat and two veg generation.

One of the joys of our annual visits to Lismore was the company of Eddie Sackville West. He preferred to live in a small house in Clogheen, fourteen miles from Lismore, rather than the vast and wonderful Knole which he inherited. Eddie was small, delicate and beautifully dressed, the model for the hypochondriac Davy in Nancy's *Love in a Cold Climate*. Before he drove over the Knockmealdown Mountains to dinner with us he used to telephone to find out if we were going to play Freda. If so, he would bring a change of clothes. Freda is a game round the billiard table. It is very quiet compared to the energetic and sometimes dangerous billiard fives played with gusto by succeeding generations of Cavendishes and Cecils. Fives is the ruiner of the green cloth, the pictures and anyone in the way of the flying billiard balls. Freda hardly warrants special clothes, but Eddie was not going to risk his dinner jacket so he changed and trotted down the passage to the billiard room like an excited schoolboy.

Eddie loved Ireland with a passion, but he did not love coarsely mashed potatoes and neither do I.

Nor do I like broad beans left until they grow thick grey vests or peas as hard as golf balls. One of the reasons for having a kitchen garden (ours was made in the early 1990s) is so that we can have veg picked at the right moment and eaten the same day. I think peas and broad beans are the veg most worth growing; you cannot buy the taste and consistency they have on the one day in their lives when they reach perfection, so you must not only face the bother of growing them, but keep a hawk-like eye on their progress or the whole point is gone.

A couple of plants of Purple- and its relation White- Sprouting Early (you are supposed to know it is broccoli) produce a spring treat. I rarely see either in the shops, but there is a horrendous veg calling itself broccoli which has enormous tasteless heads like green beads. It became famous when a sensible American president announced he didn't like it and the growers created an almighty fuss. The early kinds are much smaller and both heads and stalks are very good indeed. You can cut and cut again from these obliging brassicas.

Jerusalem artichokes are a winter favourite of mine, so is celery. Unfortunately artichokes are also the pheasants' favourite – a couple of epicurean cocks can soon spoil a bed of these. The root is the best bit of celery. It is always cut off when bought, so I am afraid you must grow it too if you want that crisp mouthful. **DD**

VEGETABLE BUTTER SAUCE

This is a versatile sauce that turns any simple vegetable into something special. You can vary it by adding any chopped herbs, or pesto, or diced capers and anchovies.

725ml/1¼ pints vegetable stock (see page 30)

250g/9oz cold unsalted butter, cut into 1cm/¼in dice

a squeeze of lemon juice

flaked sea salt

freshly ground black pepper

Bring the stock to the boil and reduce to 150ml/¼ pint. Turn the heat down and whisk in the butter, dice by dice. Add a squeeze of lemon juice and season to taste. Keep warm, but do not boil or the sauce will separate. **HM**

CHATSWORTH FILLING FOR BAKED POTATOES

	NUMBER OF SERVINGS	
	12	100
cream cheese	200g/8oz	1.6kg/4lb
cottage cheese	200g/8oz	1.6kg/4lb
natural yoghurt	25ml/1fl oz	200ml/7fl oz
garlic puree	tip of a teaspoon	1 tablespoon
lemons, juice of	½ lemon	4 lemons
flaked sea salt	½ level teaspoon	4 level teaspoons
freshly ground black pepper	¼ level teaspoon	1–2 level teaspoons
parsley, freshly chopped	2 tablespoons	40g/1½oz

Mix all the ingredients together. Split open hot baked potatoes. Spoon in the mixture and serve. For extra luxury and flavour, add a knob of butter to the potato before adding the filling. **PG**

FLUFFY MASHED POTATO WITH CHEESE

SERVES 6

110g/4oz butter, plus extra for
  greasing

25g/1oz grated Parmesan

600g/1lb 5oz potatoes, cut evenly
  into 2.5cm/1in dice

1 large shallot, finely sliced

2 garlic cloves, crushed

1 bay leaf

1 sprig of fresh thyme

1 clove

a pinch of dried chilli flakes

4 eggs, separated

½ nutmeg, grated

4 spring onions or a small bunch
  of chives, finely sliced

150g/5oz mature Cheddar cheese, grated

flaked sea salt

freshly ground black pepper

Preheat the oven to 180C/350F/Gas 4. Generously butter an ovenproof dish and dust it with the Parmesan.

Put the potatoes, shallot, garlic, bay leaf, thyme, clove and chilli flakes in a pan and cover them with lightly salted cold water. Bring to the boil and simmer over a moderate heat for about 20 minutes until the potatoes are cooked through. Drain, and discard the bay leaf and thyme. Dry the potatoes on a baking tray in the oven for a few minutes, then transfer them to large pan and mash them thoroughly while they are still hot. Over a moderate heat, mix in 50g/2oz of the butter and the egg yolks, beating well with a wooden spoon. Season with salt and pepper and grated nutmeg. Cover with a lid or foil to keep warm.

Melt the remaining butter in a small pan and cook the spring onions or chives without browning until they are soft, and stir them into the potatoes.

Whisk the egg whites until they form stiff peaks. Whisk a third of the egg whites into the potato mixture to loosen it. Then, with a large metal spoon, gently fold in the remaining egg whites and two-thirds of the grated Cheddar (do not over-mix or you will knock out the air). Spoon the mixture into the prepared dish and sprinkle with the remaining Cheddar. Bake in the oven for about 45 minutes, until set and golden. **HM**

POTATOES 'BOULANGÈRE'

SERVES 6

20g/¾oz softened butter

75g/3oz clarified butter

500g/1lb 2oz onions, finely sliced

700g/1lb 8oz main crop potatoes

275ml/½ pints vegetable or white
chicken stock (see pages 27 and 30)

1 teaspoon fresh or dried thyme

1 bay leaf

1 level tablespoon flaked sea salt

½ teaspoon freshly ground pepper

2 smoked bacon rashers (about
50g/2oz)

Preheat the oven to 180C 350F Gas 4. Grease an ovenproof dish with the softened butter.

Melt the clarified butter in a pan over a moderate heat. Add the onions, season them with salt and pepper and fry until golden brown, stirring from time to time.

Cut the potatoes into 3mm/⅛in slices and put these into a large mixing bowl (do not wash them). When the onions are ready, add the stock (or water), herbs and seasoning to the pan, bring to the boil and pour over the potatoes. Mix well and spoon into the prepared dish. Lay the bacon rashers on top, cover with foil and bake for 1¾–2 hours, removing the foil after an hour. **HM**

POTATOES 'DAUPHINOIS'

This potato dish can be cooked a day or two ahead and reheated as required. You can vary it by replacing half the potatoes with celeriac or Jerusalem artichokes or parsnips. To accompany pork, you could use a third potatoes, a third celeriac and a third apples; and to accompany beef dishes you could add 3 tablepoons of creamed horseradish.

SERVES 6

1 garlic clove, lightly crushed, and
  2 garlic cloves, finely chopped
20g/¾oz softened butter
330ml/12fl oz double cream
200ml/7fl oz milk
2 teaspoons flaked sea salt

scant ½ teaspoon pepper
⅓ nutmeg, grated finely
800g/1lb 12oz main crop potatoes
25g/1oz Gruyère cheese, grated
  (optional)

Preheat the oven to 180C/350F/Gas 4. Rub the single clove of garlic over the inside of an ovenproof dish, and then grease the dish with the softened butter.

Heat the cream and milk in a large pan with the salt, pepper, nutmeg and the 2 chopped garlic cloves. Bring to a simmer and then take off the heat. Cut the potatoes into 3mm/⅛in slices (do not wash them) and add them to the hot milk and cream. Using a wooden spoon, and stirring frequently, bring the mixture quickly back to the boil and then tip it into the prepared dish and level out the potato slices. Place the dish on a baking sheet and bake for 1 hour.

Turn down the oven to 160C/325F/Gas 3. Remove the dish from the oven and, using kitchen paper, gently soak up any excess fat that has formed round the sides of the dish. Sprinkle with the Gruyère cheese, if you are using it, and return to the oven for a further 30 minutes. Check that the potatoes are cooked by inserting a knife into the centre of the dish. **HM**

ROAST POTATOES

SERVES 6

9 potatoes (preferably Marfona, Maris Piper or King Edward), each weighing about 175g/6oz

75g/3oz salt

50g/2oz dripping or lard

50g/2oz butter

flaked sea salt

freshly ground black pepper

Preheat the oven to 200C/400F/Gas 6.

Cut each potato in half across the equator, put the halves into a large pan and cover with cold water. Add the salt, bring to the boil and simmer for a few minutes. The potatoes should be soft on the outside but hard on the inside. Drain, and set aside until they are cool enough to handle.

Melt the dripping or lard and butter in a roasting tin in the oven. Once the potatoes are cool, scrape a fork over each to roughen the surface. Carefully roll each half in the melted fat, making sure that it is covered all over. Season with salt and pepper. Roast in the oven for 1 hour, turning the potatoes every 20 minutes so that they become golden brown and crunchy all over. Serve immediately. **DW**

SPINACH WITH SORREL

We use two methods for cooking spinach before adding other ingredients: if the spinach is young and tender, we leave the stalks on and stir-fry it; if it is not so tender, we remove the stalks and boil the leaves. The sorrel adds a clean, sharp citrus flavour. If sorrel is unavailable, add a drizzle of vinegar or lemon juice just before serving.

SERVES 6

3 handfuls of sorrel leaves, washed and shredded (left whole if young, and with stalks removed if older)

110g/4oz butter

4 garlic cloves, lightly crushed

175g/6oz spinach leaves per person (if you are not using the stalks, weigh after removing them), washed and drained

½ nutmeg, grated

flaked sea salt

freshly ground black pepper

Melt 25g/1oz of the butter in a small pan, add the sorrel and cook for about 1 minute until it starts to wilt. Cool, cover and refrigerate.

TO STIR-FRY THE SPINACH: melt the remaining butter in a large sauté pan over a moderate heat, add the garlic and cook for a few minutes until the butter turns rich brown. Remove the garlic, add the spinach and turn up the heat. Cook, turning the leaves over occasionally, for about 3–5 minutes until all the leaves have wilted. Add the grated nutmeg, salt and pepper. Drain in a colander and, with a slotted spoon or small plate, press out as much excess liquid as possible. Return the spinach to the sauté pan, stir in the sorrel and reheat for a minute or two before serving.

TO BOIL THE SPINACH: bring a pan of salted water to the boil, add the spinach and cook on a high heat for a few minutes until it is tender. Drain in a colander and refresh by running a steady stream of cold water over it. When the spinach is cold, drain and squeeze as dry as possible, and set aside. Melt the remaining butter in a medium sauté pan over a moderate heat, add the garlic and cook for a few minutes until the butter turns rich brown. Remove the garlic, and add the spinach, sorrel, grated nutmeg, salt and pepper and mix well. Turn over the leaves in the butter until they are heated through. HM

BAKED SAVOY CABBAGE

An aunt used to say, 'I love my coat. It looks so cheap and was so expensive.'
Like the coat, this cabbage is one of those dishes that looks horrid and is
delicious. It loses its green and white colour in the oven, when it simply sits
with a knob of butter in a casserole with the lid on. It is a hot fawn heap
when cooked, but the taste is there because it hasn't been washed away in
tipped-out water. **DD**

SERVES 8

2 Savoy cabbages, each weighing
   about 700g/1lb 8oz
350g/12oz soft butter

flaked sea salt
freshly ground black pepper

Preheat the oven to 170C/335F/Gas 3.

Trim the outer leaves from the cabbages. Cut each cabbage into
quarters across the root, so that each quarter stays together. Put these into
a large ovenproof dish. Spread the butter evenly over each cabbage quarter,
season with salt and pepper and cover with a lid or foil. Bake in the oven
for 2–2½ hours. **HM**

BAKED SQUASH

The naturally sweet taste of this dish complements lamb particularly well.

SERVES 6

6 squash, each weighing about
   250g/9oz
225g/8oz butter
about ½ teaspoon grated nutmeg

3 tablespoons chopped parsley
flaked sea salt
freshly ground black pepper

Preheat the oven to 200C/400F/Gas 6. Cut the stalk and peduncle off the top of each squash, and cut each in half across the equator. Spread 10g/½oz of the butter on each cut face, and then place the halves, skin-side down, on a baking tray. Season with nutmeg, salt and pepper and bake in the oven for 45 15 minutes, until the squash are soft enough to insert a knife into the flesh with ease. Set aside until the squash are cool enough to handle and then, with a teaspoon, remove and discard the seeds. Scoop out the flesh into a bowl, and reserve the 6 skins that have the best bowl shapes.

Turn up the oven to 220C/425F/ Gas 7.

Mash the remaining butter into the squash flesh, season to taste and add the parsley. Fill the squash skins with the flesh and bake in the oven for 10 minutes or until hot. **DW**

SLOW-BAKED TOMATOES

The tomatoes shrivel up while they are baking, but at Chatsworth we think taste is more important than appearance.

SERVES 6

12 vine-ripened tomatoes, each
  weighing about 150g/5oz, skin on
  and cut in half horizontally
2 garlic cloves, finely chopped
100ml/4fl oz olive oil

1 tablespoon sweet balsamic vinegar
1 tablespoon dried mixed herbs
flaked sea salt
freshly ground black pepper

Preheat the oven to 140C/275F/Gas 1.

Mix the tomatoes with the garlic, olive oil, vinegar, herbs and seasoning and arrange them, cut-side up, on a cooling rack. Stand the rack on a baking tray to catch any juices and bake for about 4 hours. **HM**

CARAMELISED CHICORY

This vegetable can be a trap. Endive in England is chicory, in Belgium it is vice versa. How this came about I do not know. You want not that curly-leaved salad but the glorious torpedo-shaped firm white plant, the best of winter veg. **DD**

SERVES 6

6 chicory spears
175g/6oz soft butter
juice of 2 oranges

2 tablespoons clarified butter
flaked sea salt
freshly ground black pepper

Preheat the oven to 200C/400F/Gas 6.

Smear the chicory spears all over with the soft butter. Pack them tightly into an ovenproof dish and pour the orange juice over them. Season with salt and pepper, cover with foil and bake for 1 hour.

Drain the juices and reserve them. Allow the chicory to drain on a rack. Bring the juices to the boil and cook until they are reduced to a buttery orange syrup. Set aside.

Heat the clarified butter in a frying pan until it is hot. Add the chicory and cook, turning frequently, until it is golden brown all over. Transfer it to a warm serving dish, reheat the juices and drizzle them over the chicory spears before serving. **DW**

LEEKS IN MUSTARD SAUCE

We serve this with roast or pan-fried meat dishes, and it goes especially well with lamb. Even people who are not generally fans of leeks seem to enjoy them cooked this way.

SERVES 6

700g/1lb 8oz trimmed leeks, white and green parts
75g/3oz butter
75ml/3fl oz dry white wine
200ml/7fl oz double cream

3 tablespoons ready-made English mustard
2 tablespoons chopped chives
½ tablespoon chopped tarragon
flaked sea salt
freshly ground black pepper

Cut the leeks into pieces 6cm/2½in long, then cut into 5mm/¼in strips. Rinse thoroughly in cold water, making sure you remove all traces of soil. Drain well. Melt the butter in a sauté pan over a moderate heat, add the leeks and wine and stir well. Cover with a lid and cook for 4–5 minutes until the leeks are soft, stirring from time to time. Pour in the cream, turn up the heat and boil until the cream thickens enough to coat the leeks. Add the mustard and fresh herbs, and season to taste before serving. **HM**

LETTUCE, PEA AND ONION STEW

If you do not include the bacon, this makes a good vegetarian dish.

SERVES 6

2 Little Gem lettuces
1 tablespoon butter
75g/3oz finely sliced spring onions
    or finely diced onion
75g/3oz diced bacon
1 garlic clove, finely diced
12 pickling onions or small shallots

225g/8oz petit pois or garden peas
275ml/½ pint vegetable stock (see page
    30)
flaked sea salt
freshly ground black pepper
2 tablespoons chopped parsley

Wash the lettuces, dry them in a salad spinner and shred finely. Set them aside.

Melt the butter in a pan over a low heat. Add the spring onions or diced onion, the bacon and garlic and cook gently for a few minutes. Add the pickling onions or shallots, petit pois or peas and the vegetable stock. Bring to the boil, then turn down the heat, cover, and simmer for 30 minutes.

Remove the lid, stir in the lettuce and cook for a further 10 minutes uncovered. Season to taste and add the chopped parsley before serving. **DW**

COURGETTE, TOMATO AND RED ONION GRATIN

Vegetarians must be considered. In 1963 the President of India came to stay. He ate only boiled rice and pulses, not even eggs or milk, so by Sunday night we were at a loss as to what to give him for dinner. It is not easy to ring the changes with peas, beans, lentils and rice with no chance of cheering up their taste. But his diet was his choice because of his beliefs. Luckily from the housekeeper's point of view, out-and-out vegetarians like him are few. But if one should turn up, the tomato and courgette dish is perfectly OK – just leave out the Parmesan. **DD**

SERVES 6

165ml/6fl oz virgin olive oil

450g/1lb red onions, finely sliced

2 cloves garlic, finely chopped

2 tablespoons chopped parsley

1 teaspoon dried thyme

600g/1lb 4oz courgettes, cut on the
diagonal into 5mm/¼in slices

900g/2lb vine-ripened tomatoes, skinned
and cut vertically into 5mm/¼in slices

1 teaspoon dried mixed herbs

12 black marinated olives, stoned
and cut in half

60g/2¼oz finely grated Parmesan

flaked sea salt

freshly ground black pepper

Preheat the oven to 180C/350F/Gas 4. Heat 3 tablespoons of the olive oil in a heavy-bottomed frying pan over a medium heat and add the onions. Season, and cook until they are caramelised, stirring frequently. Set aside.

Combine the garlic, parsley, thyme, mixed herbs and remaining olive oil, and divide the mixture between two bowls. Mix the tomato slices into one bowl, and the courgette slices into the other. Season well.

Spread the onions in the bottom of an ovenproof dish. Use these as a base to make alternating rows of courgette and tomato slices standing upright on their sides. Pour over the remains of the olive oil mix. Cover with foil, sealing well, and bake for about 2 hours.

Remove the foil, sprinkle with the olives and Parmesan, and return to the oven for about 40 minutes to allow the cheese to melt and form a crust. **HM**

SALAD AND SALAD DRESSINGS

Leaf salads are served at Chatsworth every day, using whatever is available from the kitchen garden. These include year-round Mizuma, Rocket, Turnip tops, Lambs lettuce, Watercress, American Land Cress, Mibuna, Purslane, and Sorrel, and more seasonal Chicory spears, Lollo rosso, Little Gems, Oak Leaves and Radicchio.

We soak the leaves for a few minutes in cold water to revive them, and then dry them well. The dressings are added at the last moment because the acidity of the vinegar alters the texture and colour of the leaves. We sometimes add a garnish, which varies from finely sliced celery or chopped shallots to chopped walnuts, or fried breadcrumbs or parsnip crisps (see pages 108–110). The following two dressings are the ones we use most often.

A DRESSING FOR MIXED OR BITTER LEAVES

150ml/5fl oz balsamic vinegar
75g/3oz muscovado sugar
1 tablespoon flaked sea salt

1 tablespoon freshly ground black pepper
2 heaped tablespoons Dijon mustard
570ml/1 pint olive oil

Warm the vinegar in a small pan, add the sugar and stir until it dissolves. Cool and stir in the salt, pepper and mustard before gradually whisking in the olive oil. Store in a bottle at room temperature and shake well before use.

A WALNUT DRESSING FOR LEAVES TO ACCOMPANY COLD ROAST GAME OR CHEESE DISHES

2 tablespoons white wine vinegar
2 teaspoons flaked sea salt
1 teaspoon freshly ground black pepper

4 tablespoons walnut oil
2 tablespoons non-scented oil (grapeseed or sunflower)

Mix all the ingredients together. Store as above. **HM**

PUDDINGS

I NOTICE THAT PEOPLE either love puddings or skip them in favour of cheese. You would never want to skip one if it was accompanied by Devonshire Cream.

Perhaps I should not include this delectable food because it is seldom possible to obtain milk 'immediately after milking'. The law decrees that milk which is to be sold should be pasteurised, homogenised and a few other -iseds, so it is usually quite old by the time it reaches a kitchen and it is certainly not there 'immediately after milking'.

We are fortunate because we have the equivalent of a house cow in our Farmyard, which was set up in 1973 to explain to visitors the lifecycles of British farmstock and their commercial uses. There is a demonstration of milking every afternoon and it is the resulting milk that we use to make Devonshire Cream.

Children are riveted by the performance and never move till forced to do so by parent or teacher. It is an eye-opener for most of the audience and they watch, fascinated, and listen in rapt attention to the commentary. One teacher told me that if she could get her pupils to be as interested in reading and writing there would be no more illiteracy. Some are shocked. I asked a little boy from a Sheffield school what he thought of it. He gave me an awful look and said, 'It's the most disgusting thing I've ever seen in me life. I'll never drink milk again.' Even some teachers are vague about this basic food. One did not know that a cow must have a calf before she will give milk.

If you are lucky enough to come by some milk straight from the cow, this is how to make Devonshire Cream:

Put the milk into a skimming pan (a large, wide pan with a lip) and leave it in a cool place for 24 hours. Then stand the skimming pan in a larger pan filled with cold water on top of the stove and heat it slowly until the milk reaches 85C or until a crinkly yellow skin forms on top. Leave it to cool for another 24 hours, then pour away all the skim milk from beneath the thick layer of cream, and – this is the real trick – gently lift out the crust in one piece without disturbing it. DD

MALVA PUDDING

Diana and Pam brought back the receipt for this pudding from a visit to South Africa. There is a drawing of a Dutch farmhouse but no name or address on the paper. I remember their enthusiasm for this, a sort of super-nursery pudding. There is none better on a winter's day in this country. **DD**

SERVES 6

375g/13oz plain flour

3 teaspoons bicarbonate of soda

25g/1oz salt

560g/1lb 4oz caster sugar

3 eggs

3 tablespoons apricot jam

500ml/18fl oz milk

3 tablespoons butter

3 teaspoons white wine vinegar

FOR THE SAUCE

250ml/9fl oz double cream

250ml/9fl oz milk

560g/1lb 4oz caster sugar

250ml/9fl oz hot water

250g/9oz butter

Preheat the oven to 190C/375F/Gas 5.

Sift the flour, bicarbonate of soda and salt together. Beat the sugar and eggs together until light and fluffy. Then beat in the apricot jam followed by the milk. Melt the butter and vinegar together and add this to the mixture. Gently fold in the flour and pour into a well-buttered pie dish. Bake in the oven for 1½ hours.

Towards the end of the cooking time, bring all the sauce ingredients to the boil in a deep pan.

When you take the pudding out of the oven, pierce it all over with a skewer and ladle over a few tablespoons of the sauce. Allow this to soak in before serving, and hand the remaining sauce separately. **DW**

CHOCOLATE FUDGE PUDDING

SERVES 6

150g/5oz chocolate (70% cocoa solids)   110g/4oz caster sugar
150g/5oz butter   4 eggs, separated
1 teaspoon pure vanilla essence   25g/1oz self-raising flour, sieved
150ml/¼ pint warm water   pinch of cream of tartar

Preheat the oven to 200C/400F/Gas 6.

Melt the chocolate and butter over a very gentle heat. Take off the heat and add the vanilla essence, warm water and caster sugar and beat with a wooden spoon until the mixture is smooth. Add the egg yolks and beat again, and then add the sieved flour.

Whisk the egg whites with a pinch of cream of tartar until they form stiff peaks, fold them gently into the chocolate mixture and pour into a greased 1.2l/2 pint pie dish.

Stand the dish in a roasting tin and pour in enough boiling water to come halfway up the sides of the dish. Cook in the oven for 40–45 minutes until the top feels firm, but the pudding is still soft and fudgy underneath.

Serve either hot or cold with thick cream. **DW**

CHOCOLATE PUDDINGS
WITH LIQUORICE SAUCE

These puddings can be prepared a day in advance, but should be cooked just before serving. The sauce can be made 2–3 hours ahead and kept warm. Liquorice sticks are available from sweet shops, and liquorice root is available from health food shops. You will need one 150ml/5¼ pint foil tin per person.

	NUMBER OF SERVINGS	
	12	48
eggs	4	16
egg yolks	4	16
sugar	275g/10oz	1.1kg/2lb 8oz
butter	200g/7oz	800g/1lb 12oz
plain chocolate (70% cocoa solids)	160g/6oz	640g/1lb 8oz
plain flour	110g/4oz	450g/1lb

FOR THE SAUCE

	12	48
egg yolks	4	16
sugar	55g/2oz	220g/8oz
milk	425ml/¾ pint	1.7l/3 pints
liquorice stick, cut into small pieces	13cm/5in	50cm/20in
liquorice root, cut into small pieces	13cm/5in	50cm/20in
whipping cream	25ml/1fl oz	100ml/4fl oz

Preheat the oven to 180C/350F/Gas 4. Grease as many foil tins as you require. Whisk the eggs, yolks and sugar together until they are pale and fluffy. Melt the butter and chocolate together over a very low heat in a pan, or in a bowl over simmering water. Remove from the heat and slowly add to the egg mixture. Stir in the flour and spoon the mixture into the prepared foil tins. (At this stage the puddings can refrigerated if you do not want to cook them straightaway.) Bake in the oven for 15 minutes, until the puddings feel firm and springy to the touch.

Make the sauce by whisking the egg yolks and sugar together until they are pale and combined. Bring the milk to the boil and add the pieces of liquorice stick and root. Bring back to the boil and then set aside to infuse the liquorice root and to allow the pieces of liquorice stick to melt. Strain the milk, discard the root, and bring the milk back to the boil. Pour the milk on to the egg mixture, and stir in the cream. Continue to stir over a low heat until the sauce thickens slightly.

To serve, pour a pool of sauce on to each plate and turn the puddings out on top of this. Hand the remaining sauce separately. **PG**

STICKY TOFFEE PUDDINGS WITH BUTTERSCOTCH SAUCE

This pudding is a favourite with people of all ages. If it were dropped from the Carriage House Restaurant menu, I would get a pile of complaining letters. **DD**

The puddings and the sauce can be made a day in advance and then warmed through before serving. You will need one 150ml/¼ pint foil tin per person.

	NUMBER OF SERVINGS	
	12	48
butter, at room temperature	110g/4oz	450g/1lb
soft dark brown sugar	170g/6oz	680g/1lb 8oz
eggs, at room temperature	4	12
self-raising flour	225g/8oz	900g/2lb
dates, stoned and chopped	225g/8oz	900g/2lb
bicarbonate of soda	1 level teaspoon	3 level teaspoons
boiling water	300ml/½ pint	1.2l/2 pints
coffee essence	2 tablespoons	8 tablespoons
FOR THE TOFFEE GLAZE		
butter	55g/2oz	225g/8oz
whipping cream	1½ tablespoons	6½ tablespoons
dark brown sugar	70g/2½oz	280g/10oz
FOR THE BUTTERSCOTCH SAUCE		
butter	225g/8oz	900g/2lb
whipping cream	600ml/1 pint	2.4l/4 pints
dark brown sugar	420g/15oz	1,7kg/3lb 12oz

Preheat the oven to 190C/375F/Gas 5. Grease as many foil tins as you require.

Beat the butter and sugar together until they are pale and fluffy. Add the eggs gradually, beating well, and adding a little flour if the mixture shows signs of curdling. Fold in the flour. Put the dates and bicarbonate of soda into a bowl and cover with the boiling water for one minute (to soften the dates). Add the dates and water and the coffee essence to the mixture and stir well. Divide among the tins and bake in the oven for 45 minutes–1 hour, until the puddings are firm and springy to the touch.

Make the glaze and the sauce in two separate pans. The method is the same for both: melt the butter, add the other ingredients and stir until the sugar is dissolved and the mixture is hot. Set aside and keep warm.

When the puddings are cooked, turn them out on to a serving dish, stab holes all over them with a skewer and pour over the toffee glaze, allowing it to soak in for a minute or two. If you have time, put the puddings under a grill for a few moments – this will make them even stickier. Then pour the butterscotch sauce over the puddings and serve immediately. **PG**

GUARDS PUDDING

SERVES 6

75g/3oz butter, at room temperature
50g/2oz caster sugar
1 x 350g/12oz jar of good quality
  strawberry jam
2 eggs, beaten, at room temperature

150g/5oz fresh breadcrumbs (brioche
  if possible)
1 teaspoon bicarbonate of soda
75ml/3fl oz dark rum

Beat the butter and sugar together until pale and fluffy. Beat in 3 tablespoons of the jam. Slowly add the eggs, beating well between each addition. Stir in the breadcrumbs and bicarbonate of soda, and pour into a well-greased 1.2l/2 pint basin and cover tightly with foil. Steam for 1¼ hours.

Make the sauce by heating the remaining jam and the rum together until boiling, and then straining it through a fine sieve into a clean pan. Reserve the strawberry pulp.

When the pudding is cooked, turn it out, place the pulp on top and drizzle a little sauce all over it. Hand the remaining sauce separately. **DW**

THE DUKE'S BREAD AND BUTTER PUDDING

Many English dishes surprise French people, but they are astonished by our liberal use of bread. I know they have pain perdue *but look at our list – fried bread with eggs and bacon at breakfast, bread sauce with roast chicken, fried breadcrumbs in yet another sauce boat with game, brown bread ice cream, the incomparable summer pudding and, best of all in the winter, bread and butter pudding.* DD

SERVES 6

25g/1oz sultanas

25g/1oz butter

4 thin slices of white bread, crusts removed

2 eggs

50g/2oz caster sugar

150ml/¼ pint double cream

150ml/¼ pint milk

1 vanilla pod, split

2 tablespoons marmalade

Preheat the oven to190C/375F/Gas 5. Cover the sultanas with boiling water and leave to soak for about 10 minutes. Butter the slices of bread, cut them into triangles and place in a 570ml/1 pint dish.

Whisk the eggs and sugar together until pale and thick. Pour the cream and milk into a pan, add the vanilla pod, and bring to the boil. Stir a little of the creamy milk into the egg mixture, then whisk in the remainder. Scrape all the seeds from the vanilla pod and add these to the milk and egg mixture. (Rinse and dry the pod for use in another dish.) Pour over the bread and dot the drained sultanas over the top.

Stand the dish in a roasting tin and pour in enough boiling water to come halfway up the sides of the dish. Cook in the oven for 40–45 minutes. As soon as you take the pudding out of the oven, spread the marmalade over the top and leave it to rest for 10 minutes before serving. DW

MACAROON LEMON POSSET

Left-over macaroons can be used in other ways. We sandwich them together with a dessertspoon of good quality apricot jam, or coffee- or chocolate-flavoured buttercream and leave them in an airtight container for 2–3 days so that they are soft and chewy, for afternoon tea.

SERVES 6

**FOR THE MACAROONS
(MAKES ABOUT 20)**
60g/2½oz ground almonds
125g/4½oz caster sugar
1 tablespoon ground rice (fine)
2 egg whites
a few drops of vanilla essence
almond flakes for decoration

FOR THE POSSET
425ml/¾ pint double cream
juice and grated zest of 1½ unwaxed
  lemons
125g/4½oz caster sugar
1 tablespoon rum

Start by making the macaroons. Preheat the oven to 180C/350F/Gas 4. Line two baking trays with silicone paper.

To make the macaroons, combine the dry ingredients and stir in the egg whites and vanilla essence. Using a 1cm/½in plain nozzle, pipe the mixture on to the trays in small mounds of about 2.5cm/1in in diameter, leaving a space between each one because they will spread. Place a few almond flakes on each and bake in the oven for about 25 minutes. The macaroons harden as they cool down so, using a palette knife, transfer them to a cooling rack as soon as you take them out of the oven.

To make the posset, combine the cream, grated lemon zest and caster sugar in a pan and bring to the boil for a minute. Take off the heat and stir in the lemon juice and rum. Strain the mixture into a jug to remove the lemon zest.

Place a macaroon in each of six 100ml/4fl oz ramekins, and pour over the posset mixture, filling each ramekin to the top. Cool and refrigerate for 2–3 hours to set and chill. **HM**

PEPPERED BAKED PEARS
WITH MARSALA SABAYON

The pears can be served simply with thick, slightly sweetened cream, but the sabayon sauce makes them very special. The best combination of all is the sauce and vanilla ice cream – this gives a contrast of temperature as well as sweetness. Once cold, the sauce can also be served as an alternative to cream with any red summer fruit. The vanilla pods can be washed, dried at room temperature, and either used again or added to stored sugar to flavour it.

SERVES 6

1 orange

3 large ripe pears (preferably Conference, Williams or Packhams Triumph), each weighing about 200g/7oz

110g/4oz butter

40g/1½oz clear honey

25g/1oz light muscovado sugar

1 vanilla pod, split in half

½ tablespoon grated fresh ginger

½ teaspoon five spices or mixed spices

110ml/4fl oz ginger wine

55ml/2fl oz dry white wine

12 green peppercorns (bottled or canned)

pepper mill filled with black peppercorns

25g/1oz toasted flaked almonds

FOR THE SABAYON SAUCE

5 egg yolks

85g/3½ oz caster sugar or light muscavado sugar

½ teaspoon vanilla extract

75ml/3fl oz Marsala

275ml/½ pint double cream

Start by making the sauce. Find a heatproof bowl that fits over a pan of boiling water without the bottom touching the water. Bring 7.5cm/3in of water to a simmer in the pan while you whisk the egg yolks, sugar, vanilla extract and Marsala together in the bowl. When the mixture is pale yellow and foamy, place the bowl over the simmering water, and continue to whisk until the mixture thickens, increases in volume, and becomes creamy in texture. It is ready when it leaves clear ribbon trails when you lift the whisk.

While whisking, test the temperature of the sabayon with your finger from time to time; if it feels hotter than tepid, remove the bowl from the simmering water and whisk away from the heat. When the sabayon is ready, take it off the heat and stand the bowl in very cold water, whisking intermittently until the sauce is cold. Whip the cream until it forms soft peaks and gently fold it into the sauce.

Before you start to prepare the pears, preheat the oven to 180C/350F/Gas 4.

Pare the zest from the orange in wide strips, using a potato peeler. Squeeze the juice from the orange and reserve it. Peel the pears and cut each in half lengthways. Core the pears (a melon baller makes this easier) and remove any tough threads that run from the top of the core to the stalk.

Melt 50g/2oz of the butter in a heavy ovenproof frying or sauté pan over a medium heat. Add the honey, sugar, five spices or mixed spice, orange zest and ginger, stir until dissolved and add the vanilla pod. Add the pears, rolling them in the mixture and cooking them for about 2 minutes before positioning them, cut-sides down in the pan. Add the orange juice, ginger wine, white wine and green peppercorns, and sprinkle 3 turns of the peppermill over each pear half. Bring to the boil, and then transfer the pan to the oven. Cook for about 25 minutes or until the pears are soft and slightly caramelised, basting with the juices from time to time.

Lift the pears on to a warm serving dish and remove the vanilla pod and orange zest. Reheat the pear juices, whisk in the remaining butter and pour over the pears. Serve sprinkled with a few toasted flaked almonds, and hand the sauce separately. **HM**

APPLE PARCELS
WITH TOFFEE AND WHISKY SAUCE

The parcels can be prepared a day in advance, but are better if they are actually cooked just before serving. The sauce can be made a day in advance. You will find it easier to form the parcels with a mould 9cm/3½in in diameter and 4cm/1½in deep, but you do only need one of these. For 96 people, double the quantities for 48.

	NUMBER OF SERVINGS	
	12	48
clarified butter	350g/12oz	1.4kg/3lb
Cox's apples, peeled, cored and thickly sliced	12	48
caster sugar	150g/6oz	600g/1lb 8oz
whisky	50ml/2fl oz	225ml/8fl oz
melted butter for brushing pastry	250g/8oz	1kg/2lb
sheets of filo pastry, each 15cm/6in square	48	192
icing sugar for dusting	2 tablespoons	8 tablespoons
FOR THE TOFFEE AND WHISKY SAUCE		
caster sugar	425g/15oz	1.7kg/3lb 12oz
double cream	150ml/¼ pint	600ml/1 pint
whisky	275ml/9fl oz	1.1l/1¾ pint

Start by making the sauce. Make it in batches, in quantities for 12 people at a time. Put the sugar in a heavy-bottomed pan over a medium heat, without any water, stirring from time to time until the sugar turns to a medium-brown caramel. Take off the heat and immediately add the cream, followed by the whisky – take care that the mixture does not spit on to your hands. Now return the pan to a low heat and stir until the hardened caramel dissolves. Set aside and keep warm, or cool and reheat later

Cook the apples in small batches of 4 apples at a time. For each batch, melt 100g/4oz of the clarified butter in a large pan over a medium heat, and cook the apples. When the slices start to colour on both sides, sprinkle on 50g/2oz of the sugar. When the sugar starts to caramelise, add a third of the whisky (about a tablespoon) and set it alight with a match to flambé it. Then remove immediately from the heat – do not overcook.

Preheat the oven to 190C/375F/Gas 5. Butter one side of a filo square. Butter the top of a second and place it on the first one, at 45 degrees so that you end up with 8 corners. Then add a third piece, also at an angle, but do not butter this one. Lift the pastry into a mould so it overlaps the edges. Layer the apples inside, but do not fill the parcel too high. Fold in the sides to seal the parcel and butter the pastry all over. Now carefully tip the parcel out on to a greased baking tray with the edges facing up, but make sure the parcel stays closed. (You may find it easiest to tip it first into the palm of your hand and then out on to the tray.) Butter the parcel again. Take a fourth piece of pastry, scrunch it up, and place it on top of the parcel as decoration and brush it with butter. Repeat for all the parcels.

Cook for 20 minutes. When the parcels are nicely browned, place each one on a plate, dust with icing sugar and serve with the sauce around the parcel. **PG**

APPLE COMPOTE
WITH BLACK TREACLE AND
DEVONSHIRE CREAM

This is all a pudding should be – sweet, sour and creamy. Black treacle is the same thing as molasses – good for horses and for us. **DD**

SERVES 6–8

1.1kg/2lb 8oz Bramley or other
    cooking apples, peeled, cored and
    roughly chopped
250g/9oz caster sugar
1 cinnamon stick
1 vanilla pod
juice of 1 lemon
5 Russet or other firm eating apples

TO SERVE
black treacle, warmed
Devonshire Cream or thick double
    cream

Preheat the oven to 180C/350F/Gas 4.

Put the Bramley apples, sugar, cinnamon stick, vanilla pod and lemon juice in a large pan over a gentle heat and cook until the apples are reduced to a purée, stirring from time to time. Meanwhile, peel and core the eating apples and cut each into 16 pieces. Place these in an ovenproof dish, pour over the purée, and bake for 30 minutes. The pieces of eating apple should be soft but still keep their shape.

Take out the cinnamon stick and vanilla pod, and serve the apple compote hot or at room temperature with the black treacle and cream. **DW**

BREADS, BISCUITS & CAKES

B READ WAS A PASSION of my mother and her siblings. In Mrs Alhusen's book there is a long receipt for bread made of English stoneground wholemeal flour, including detailed descriptions of the utensils to be used. My interest quickened when I turned the page and saw the name of the contributor – Mr Geoffrey Bowles.

He was my uncle and a true eccentric if ever there was one. He never married and lived alone in one of those delectable houses in Catherine Street, Westminster. Visitors were not allowed. Should you be bold enough to ring the bell, he opened a flap in the door to tell you to go away. His sister, my aunt, lived near by. When they were old and she hadn't seen him for a long time, she thought she would like to do so and wrote to suggest that they should meet. 'But we *have* met,' he replied. For years Uncle Geoff lived on nothing but chocolate, which he bought at Fortnum & Mason, and bread, which he made himself. 'The perfect diet,' he said.

My mother campaigned against white bread and conducted a vendetta against the Wicked Millers, headed in her opinion by Lord Rank, through letters to the papers and talks to the local Women's Institutes. She vowed that they made fortunes by extracting the germ of the wheat (the nutritious part) to sell as a 'health food' and that the outer case of the grain, bran, was also separated for the same commercial purpose, leaving lifeless, tasteless white flour with no goodness in it, steamed not baked, to make bread a staple food for the unsuspecting population. She held that whole grain ground between stones contains all the necessary ingredients to deserve the name 'the Staff of Life'. No wonder Uncle Geoff thrived on it.

White bread was not allowed in our house. We longed for it, of course (as we longed for shop butter instead of the superb butter made in our own dairy from the milk of Guernsey cows). Now I want the authentic taste of my mother's bread, nutty and different from any of the fantastic variety of loaves of all nations to be found in every supermarket. It keeps, and even improves, for eight or nine days, so it need only be made once a week. And, of course, it freezes perfectly. Her receipt is given overleaf.

Give this receipt to two people and, like singing a song, the result will not be exactly the same. Perhaps that is because the yeast it includes is live and almost kicking, making the dough rise and take on another shape. My mother bought this vital agent from the Postal Yeast Company, Leeds – the name and address is etched in my memory because it was printed on a tie-on label, much bigger than the squashy little parcel itself. It arrived weekly in our house and was immediately put to use.

I wish I liked cakes. I see them eaten by others with joy but somehow I can't get up enthusiasm for them, with the exception of those given here.

Crisp, savoury biscuits are another matter. Some years ago a friend gave me a basket to add to a collection that spills over cupboards and shelves and litters the floor. This was no ordinary basket, not a flimsy thing of foreign ancestry which comes to bits as soon as it is used, but an object of beauty, grown and woven in Somerset. It is oval with low sides. In order that I might see it every day it is used for biscuits, which suit its make and shape. What sort of biscuits? I remembered thin, blistered, easily broken water biscuits in a friend's house. No professional baker would make them, as breakages are inevitable, and fragments have to be thrown away again and again. But in your own house such niceties don't matter. I think we have perfected this brittle accompaniment to other food. Judging by the handfuls taken from the basket every day, other people think so too.

Its basket-fellows are equally popular biscuits I have not met elsewhere. **DD**

MY MOTHER'S BREAD

MAKES 2 X 450G/1LB LOAVES

25g/1oz fresh yeast

570ml/1 pint lukewarm water

225g/8oz strong white flour

675g/1lb 8oz wholemeal flour

3 teaspoons salt

6 teaspoons light muscovado sugar

Start by crumbling the yeast into half the water in a jug and leave to stand in a warm place for about 10 minutes.

Grease and flour two 450g/1lb loaf tins.

Mix the flours, salt and sugar together in a large bowl, and make a well in the centre. Once the yeast mix starts to bubble and fizz, add it to the flour. Start to combine the flour and yeast mixture with your hands, and then while you continue to mix with one hand, slowly pour in the rest of the water with the other hand. Mix and knead with both hands until a dough is formed. Turn it out of the bowl on to a floured surface and continue to knead for 5–6 minutes until the dough is smooth. Return the dough to the bowl, cover with clingfilm and leave it to 'prove' or rise in a warm, draught-proof place for about an hour until the dough has doubled in volume. 'Knock it back' by punching it down with your hands and kneading for 4–5 minutes. Divide the dough into two and put it into the prepared loaf tins (the dough should fill just over half the tin). Cover the tins with a clean tea towel and leave the dough to rise for another 30 minutes until it has doubled in size again.

Meanwhile preheat the oven to 200C/400F/Gas 6. When the dough has risen, bake for 35–40 minutes. Test to see if the bread is cooked by taking a loaf out of the tin and tapping the bottom of the loaf. If it sounds hollow, it is ready. If it not, put it back for another few minutes. Turn out on to a wire rack to cool.

This bread is best left for a day or two before being eaten. It can also be frozen for up to 3 months. DW

RYE BREAD

MAKES 2 X 450G/1LB LOAVES

20g/¾oz fresh yeast
350ml/12fl oz lukewarm water
275g/10oz rye flour
150g/5oz strong white flour
150g/5oz wholemeal flour
2 teaspoons salt
1 tablespoon muscovado sugar
75g/3oz black treacle
1 tablespoon oil or melted butter

FOR THE GLAZE AND
TOPPING
1 tablespoon potato flour
2 tablespoons boiling water
1 tablespoon sesame seeds
1 tablespoon pumpkin seeds
1 tablespoon sunflower seeds

Start by crumbling the yeast into half the water in a jug and leaving it to stand in a warm place for about 10 minutes.

Grease and flour two 450g/1lb loaf tins.

Mix the flours together in a bowl. Add the salt, sugar, treacle and oil or butter and stir until they are incorporated into the flour. Add the rest of the water to the yeast mix. Make a well in the middle of the flour and add half the yeast liquid. Start to combine the flour and water with your hands, and while you continue to mix with one hand, slowly pour in the rest of the yeast liquid with the other hand. Mix and knead with both hands until a dough is formed. Turn it out of the bowl on to a floured surface and continue to knead for 5–6 minutes until the dough is smooth. Return the dough to the bowl, cover with clingfilm and leave it to 'prove' or rise in a warm, draught-proof place for about an hour until the dough has doubled in volume. 'Knock it back' by punching it down with your hands and kneading for another 4–5 minutes. Divide the dough into two and put it into the prepared loaf tins (the dough should fill just over half the tin). Cover the tins with a clean tea towel and leave the dough to rise for a further 30 minutes until it has doubled in size again.

Preheat the oven to 180C/350F/Gas 4. When the dough has risen, mix the potato flour with the boiling water and gently brush on to the top of the loaves. Sprinkle over the mixed seeds. Bake for 40–45 minutes. Test to see if the bread is cooked by taking a loaf out of the tin and tapping the bottom of the loaf. If it sounds hollow, it is ready. If it not, put it back for another few minutes. Turn out on to a rack and leave to cool.

The bread can be eaten fresh, or frozen for up to 3 months. **DW**

SODA BREAD

I know soda bread is universal, but it is Irish to me and takes me straight back to tea at Lismore, sitting in the window with the formidable drop to the River Blackwater below. It should be freshly made, like scones, and its shape makes you want to cut it. This receipt is from Kathleen Penny. **DD**

Soda bread is yeast-free and does not need to be left to rise, so it is quick and simple to make. Bicarbonate of soda starts to work as soon as it is mixed with the buttermilk, so the faster you can get the dough into the oven, the better.

MAKES ONE 900G/2LB ROUND LOAF

275g/10oz self-raising flour	275g/10oz wholemeal flour
1½ teaspoons salt	1 teaspoon brown sugar
1½ teaspoons bicarbonate of soda	425ml/¾ pints buttermilk

Preheat the oven to 200C/400F/Gas 6. Grease and flour a baking tray.

Sieve the self-raising flour, salt and bicarbonate of soda together. Add the wholemeal flour and sugar, and then the buttermilk and knead until a soft dough is formed. Turn out on to a floured surface and form into a round bun shape. Place on the prepared tray and score into quarters with a sharp, floured knife, cutting about a quarter of the way through the dough. Bake for about 35–40 minutes or until the loaf sounds hollow when tapped on the bottom. Leave to cool on a rack and eat the same day. **DW**

SCONES

MAKES 12-15 SCONES

225g/8oz self-raising flour
½ teaspoon baking powder
a pinch of salt
50g/2oz butter

1 tablespoon sugar
50g/2oz sultanas (optional)
1 egg, beaten
150ml/¼ pint milk

Preheat the oven to 220C/425F/Gas 7 and line or grease a baking tray.

Sift the flour, baking powder and salt together. Rub in the butter with your fingertips until the mixture resembles fine breadcrumbs. Stir in the sugar and, if you are using them, the sultanas. Beat the egg and the milk together, pour into the crumble and mix to a soft dough.

Roll out the dough to a thickness of 2cm/¾in on a lightly floured surface. Using a pastry cutter or the rim of a glass, stamp out 5cm/2in circles, re-rolling the trimmings to use all the dough. Lift the scones on to the prepared tray, brush the tops with milk and bake for 15–20 minutes until they are well-risen and golden.

Serve the scones warm with butter and strawberry jam, or let them cool and fill them with thick, fresh cream and jam. **DW**

CHEDDAR CHEESE BISCUITS

MAKES 40 BISCUITS

150g/5oz plain flour

50g/2oz self-raising flour

110g/4oz butter

110g/4oz Cheddar cheese, grated

2 tablespoons grated Parmesan

½ teaspoon salt

¼ teaspooon cayenne pepper

juice of ½ lemon

Put all ingredients into a bowl and blend, by hand or in a processor, until they form a dough. Roll the dough into a 4cm/1½in cylinder. Wrap in clingfilm and chill in the fridge for 2 hours to firm the dough up.

Preheat the oven to 200C/400F/Gas 6. Line two baking trays with greaseproof paper.

Once the dough is firm, cut it into 5mm/¼in slices and place these on the prepared trays. Bake for 7 minutes and then flip them over and bake for a further 7 minutes or until golden brown. Cool on a wire rack. **DW**

CURRIED CHEESE BISCUITS

MAKES 30 BISCUITS

150g/5oz plain flour

110g/4oz butter

110g/4oz Chedddar cheese, grated

2 teaspoons medium curry paste
(stronger if you prefer)

a pinch of salt

¼ teaspooon finely ground pepper

desiccated coconut to coat the
biscuits

Preheat the oven to 200C/400F/Gas 6. Line two baking trays with grease-proof paper.

Put all the ingredients (except the coconut) into a bowl and blend, by hand or in a processor, until a soft dough is formed Chill in the fridge for 15–20 minutes to firm the dough up.

Scoop up enough dough to form a 2.5cm/1in ball. Roll this in the coconut so that it is well coated. Repeat until all the dough is used. Arrange the balls on the prepared baking trays, and then flatten them to small circles about 1cm/½in thick. Bake in the oven for 7 minutes and then flip them over and cook for a further 7 minutes. Cool on a wire rack. **DW**

BLUE CHEESE BISCUITS

MAKES 30 BISCUITS

150g/5oz self-raising flour

150g/5oz butter

150g/5oz Roquefort or Stilton cheese
(or a mixture of both), crumbled

a pinch of salt

¼ teaspooon finely ground pepper

sesame seeds to coat the biscuits

These are made in exactly the same way as Curried Cheese Biscuits. **DW**

WATER BISCUITS

These thin, crisp biscuits are best made using a pasta machine, but it is perfectly possible to roll out the pastry by hand, and although you will not be able to make the biscuits quite so thin, they will taste the same.

MAKES ABOUT 50 BISCUITS

275g/10oz plain flour, plus
  extra for rolling out
a pinch of salt

¼ teaspooon of finely ground pepper
3 tablespoons olive oil
110ml/4fl oz water

Rub the flour, salt, pepper and oil together with your fingers until the oil has been absorbed into the flour and the flour looks slightly coloured. Add the water and mix until a soft dough is formed. Wrap this in clingfilm and leave to rest for 10 minutes in the fridge.

Preheat the oven to 190C/375F/Gas 5. Line two baking trays with grease-proof paper.

Split the dough into 6 equal pieces. Form one of the pieces into a thin sausage and flatten it with the palm of your hand.

If you are using a pasta machine, start on the first setting, and roll the dough through, then repeat until you have rolled it through all of the settings. You may find halfway through you that have to dust the dough lightly with flour to prevent it from sticking.

If you are using a rolling pin, roll the dough out as thin as you can – ideally until the dough looks slightly transparent – on a floured surface. If you can't roll it out as thin as this, don't worry, the biscuits will be fine if they are little thicker; they will just need a few more minutes to cook.

Cut the dough into roughly square or triangular shapes, keeping the size of the biscuits to about 5cm/2in. A pizza cutter may help you do this because it is more fluent than a knife. Place the biscuits on the tray.

Repeat with the other 5 pieces of dough. Bake for 10–12 minutes, until the biscuits are golden brown all over. Cool on a wire rack. **DW**

SESAME BISCUITS

MAKES ABOUT 30 BISCUITS

150g/5 oz plain flour

60g/2½oz sesame seeds

a pinch of salt

¼ teaspooon of finely ground pepper

2 tablespoons sesame seed oil

65ml/2½fl oz water

flour for rolling out

These are made in exactly the same way as Water Biscuits. **HM**

OATMEAL SQUARES

MAKES 30 BISCUITS

275g/10oz medium oatmeal

½ teaspoon bicarbonate of soda

35g/1½oz butter

55ml/2fl oz boiling water

flour for rolling out

Preheat the oven to 200C/400F/Gas 6. Line two baking trays with grease-proof paper.

Mix the oatmeal and bicarbonate of soda and rub in the butter with your fingers until the mixture resembles wholemeal breadcrumbs. Stir in the boiling water with a fork. The mixture will be very loose at first, but after a minute or two the oatmeal will absorb the water and swell to form a dough.

Turn the dough on to a well-floured surface. First flatten the mixture with your hands – the edges will begin to crack, but just push them back together. Then dredge the surface with more flour and roll out to a thickness of 5mm/¼in. Cut the dough into 2.5cm/1in squares. Using a palette knife, ease them off the surface and place on the trays. Push the trimmings back together, adding a drop or two of water to help bind them, and then roll out as before.

Bake for 12–15 minutes or until the edges are toasted brown in colour and the centre of the biscuit feels firm if you press it. Leave to cool on the tray. **DW**

SHORTBREAD

MAKES ABOUT 24 BISCUITS

175g/6oz butter, at room
   temperature, plus extra for greasing
110g/4oz golden caster sugar or light
   muscovado sugar
a pinch of salt

a drop of vanilla extract
200g/7oz plain flour
50g/2oz cornflour
caster sugar for dusting

Start preparing these biscuits about 5 hours before you bake them, in order to allow the dough to rest for a total of about 4 hours.

Lightly grease a baking tray, or line a baking tray with greaseproof paper.

Cream the butter and sugar together with the salt and vanilla essence until pale and fluffy. Sieve in the flour and cornflour and mix as little as possible to combine all the ingredients. Scoop the sticky dough out on to a sheet of clingfilm placed on a tray, cover this with another sheet of clingfilm and, using a rolling pin, roll the dough out to a thickness of 2.5cm/1in. Leave to rest in the fridge for 2 hours.

Once the resting time is over, allow the dough to return to room temperature. Remove the top sheet of clingfilm, turn the dough out on a floured surface, remove the second sheet of clingfilm and knead the dough gently to soften it. Roll it out to a thickness of either 5mm/¼in or 8mm/⅓in, depending on whether you want thin, crunchy biscuits, or thicker, denser ones. Cut the dough into shapes of your choice, using either a pre-formed cutter or a knife, and lift on to the prepared baking tray. Rest in the refrigerator for a further 2 hours.

Preheat the oven to 150C/300F/Gas 2.

Bake until the biscuits are a very light golden colour. This will take about 20 minutes if you have made thin biscuits, or 25 minutes if you have made thicker ones. Cool on a wire rack and dust with caster sugar. **HM**

NEAPOLITAN CAKE

This comes from my mother's old receipt book. It could just as well be served as a pudding. The same Mark whom my father pressed to eat brains for breakfast dreamed of it when in a prisoner-of-war camp. No wonder. DD

The cake is built up from six thin rounds of biscuit sandwiched together with jam. It can be eaten straightaway, but it is best after a couple of days when the jam has softened the biscuit, making it moist and easier to cut.

SERVES 6-8

175g/6oz butter
75g/3oz caster sugar
175g/6oz plain flour
75g/3oz ground almonds
4 drops of almond essence (optional)

FOR THE FILLING
275g/10oz apricot jam
25g/1oz ground almonds

Preheat the oven to 190C/375F/Gas 5. Grease two large baking trays and line them with baking parchment.

Beat or process all the biscuit ingredients until they form a soft dough. Divide the mixture into 6 equal pieces. Take the ring from a loose-bottomed 15cm/6in cake tin, place it on one of the baking trays and use it as a guide to flatten and shape one portion of dough. Remove the ring, leaving the circle of dough on the tray. Repeat this process with the remaining dough. Bake for 15 minutes or until golden brown, then remove from the oven and leave to cool on the trays.

To assemble the cake, put ½ teaspoon of jam in the centre of a plate and lay one of the biscuit circles on top. (The jam will stop the cake from moving.) Spread the biscuit with about 1½ tablespoons of jam, and continue to layer the biscuits spreading jam between each. Spread a thin layer of jam on the top biscuit and coat it with ground almonds. DW

THE DUKE'S CHOCOLATE CAKE

I first tasted this chocolate cake in Washington. 'You must try this,' my hostess said. 'It was made by a Russian woman who arrived in America with nothing but this recipe and it has kept her ever since.' No wonder – it is a marvel. It is Andrew's favourite and now it seems to belong to him. DD

SERVES 6–8

110g/4oz butter

50g/2oz plain chocolate (70% cocoa
  solids)

2 eggs, beaten

225g/8oz caster sugar

50g/2oz plain flour

1 teaspoon baking powder

¼ teaspoon salt

75g/3oz ground almonds

½ teaspoon grated nutmeg

2 tablespoons Tia Maria or brandy
  (optional)

cocoa powder for dusting

FOR THE MOUSSE FILLING

50g/2oz chocolate (70% cocoa
  solids)

2 eggs, separated

25g/1oz caster sugar

FOR THE COATING

110g/4oz chocolate (70% cocoa
  solids)

220ml/4fl oz double cream

Preheat the oven to 180C/350F/Gas 4. Grease a rectangular baking tin measuring 30 x 20cm/12 x 8in and line it with baking parchment.

Start by making the cake base. Melt the butter and chocolate together in a bowl set over a pan of simmering water. Stir the mixture well and take it off the heat. Let it cool slightly and then beat in the eggs. Combine the sugar, flour, baking powder, salt, ground almonds and nutmeg. Pour the chocolate mixture into the dry ingredients and beat them together. Pour into the prepared tin and bake for about 20–25 minutes or until set. To test, give the tin a small shake and if there is no movement, it is ready (do not wait until a skewer comes out clean; by then it will be overcooked). Remove from the oven and leave to cool in the tin.

Next make the mousse filling. Melt the chocolate in a bowl over simmering water and when it has cooled slightly, beat in the egg yolks. Whisk the egg whites until fluffy, add the sugar and whisk until they hold soft peaks. Fold a tablespoon of the egg whites into the chocolate mixture to loosen it and then, using a large metal spoon, fold in the rest of the egg whites. Set aside in the fridge.

When the cake base is cold, cut it horizontally into two equal halves. At this stage you can drizzle the Tia Maria or brandy on to the halves for extra flavour. Spread the mousse evenly over one half and place the other half on top. Chill in the fridge for about 10 minutes to set.

To make the coating, melt the chocolate in a bowl over simmering water, and when it has cooled slightly, whisk in the cream to form a paste. Spread this evenly over the top and sides of the cake. Return to the fridge for 20 minutes to set.

Before serving, sieve a heavy coating of cocoa powder over the top of the cake. **DW**

GINGER CAKE

This makes a dark, rich ginger cake, which can also be served with whipped cream as a pudding. It keeps well and tastes better after three or four days. If you do not like the idea of a strong-tasting, gooey cake, which will almost certainly sink in the middle, cut the quantity of treacle to 200g/7oz. Adding 25g/1oz of coarsely chopped walnuts with the ginger and sultanas will give an agreeable bite to the cake.

SERVES 6-8

110g/4oz butter, at room temperature

110g/4oz Barbados or demerara sugar

2 eggs, at room temperature

275g/10oz black treacle

225g/8oz plain flour

1 teaspoon ground ginger

50g/2oz sultanas

½ teaspoon bicarbonate of soda

2 tablespoons lukewarm milk

Preheat the oven to 170C/325F/Gas 3. Grease a 18cm/7in cake tin and line it with baking parchment.

Cream the butter, add the sugar and continue beating for a few moments. Mix in the eggs and treacle. Sift the flour and ginger together, then stir in the sultanas and tip this into the egg mixture. Stir the bicarbonate of soda into the warm milk and mix that in last of all.

Pour into the prepared tin and bake for 1½ hours if you like a moist, sticky gingerbread, or for 1¾ hours if you like it a little drier. The cake is ready when it starts to shrink away from the sides of the tin. Let it cool for about 10 minutes in the tin, then turn it out on to a wire rack. It may sink in the middle as it cools. **DW**

CARROT CAKE

This is called Passionate Carrot Cake in the Farm Shop. The optional ingredient, glycerine, helps to keep the cake moist and is available from chemists' shops

MAKES A 700G/1½LB CAKE

75g/3oz self-raising flour

½ teaspoon mixed spice

½ teaspoon baking powder

20g/¾oz ground almonds

100g/4oz caster sugar

100g/4oz butter, at room temperature

1 teaspoon glycerine (optional)

2 medium eggs, at room temperature

150g/5oz grated carrots

50g/2oz flaked hazelnuts

50g/2oz sultanas

grated zest of ½ orange

FOR THE CIDER BRANDY BUTTER TOPPING

75g/3oz butter

75g/3oz icing sugar

35ml/1½fl oz Somerset cider brandy

grated zest of 1 unwaxed lemon

Preheat the oven to 180C/350F/Gas 4. Grease a 15cm/6in round cake tin (or equivalent) and line it with baking parchment.

Sift the flour, mixed spice and baking powder together and stir in the ground almonds.

In another bowl, beat the sugar, butter and glycerine, if you are using it, together until pale and fluffy. Beat the eggs and add them a little at a time, beating until smooth. Then fold in the flour mixture, the carrots, hazelnuts, sultanas and orange zest. Spoon the mixture into the prepared tin and bake for 50 minutes. It is cooked when a skewer inserted into the centre of the cake comes out clean. Allow to cool in the tin.

Meanwhile, make the topping by beating the butter and icing sugar together until pale and fluffy, then slowly add the cider brandy while continuing to beat. Spread this over the top of the cooled cake and sprinkle with the lemon zest. **AB**

LEMON DRIZZLE CAKE

An optional ingredient for this cake is glycerine, which helps to keep the cake moist and is available from chemists' shops.

MAKES A 400G/14OZ CAKE

100g/4oz caster sugar

100g/4oz butter, at room temperature

2 eggs, beaten, at room temperature

50g/2oz lemon curd

grated zest of 1 unwaxed lemon

½ teaspoon glycerine (optional)

35g/1½oz strong white flour

75g/3oz self-raising flour

½ teaspoon baking powder

FOR THE DRIZZLE

50g/2oz caster sugar

75ml/3fl oz lemon juice (1 large
    or 2 small lemons)

Preheat the oven to 165C/325F/Gas 3. Grease and line a 15 x 6cm/6 x 2½in loaf tin. Sift the flours and baking powder together.

Beat the sugar and butter together until light and fluffy. Beat in the eggs, a little at a time, adding a teaspoon of flour between additions if the mixture shows signs of curdling. Add the lemon curd and zest, and glycerine if you are using it, and beat together until smooth. Fold in the flours and baking powder, pour into the prepared tin and bake for about 35 minutes. The cake is cooked when a skewer inserted into its centre comes out clean.

Meanwhile, make the drizzle by mixing together the sugar and lemon juice. When you take the cake out of the oven, prick it all over the top with a skewer, drizzle over the sugar and lemon mixture, and leave to cool in the tin. **AB**

CHERRY AND ALMOND CAKE

Jean-Pierre named this 'The Duke's Favourite'. It is true that Andrew has a passion for it, and he can't understand how the cherries remain on the top. **DD**

You will need one 23cm/9in cake tin for 12 servings.

	NUMBER OF SERVINGS	
	12	48
whole glacé cherries	450g/1lb	1.8kg/4lb
self-raising flour	100g/4oz	450g/1lb
salt	¼ teaspoon	2 teaspoons
ground almonds	150g/5oz	600g/1lb 4oz
butter, at room temperature	200g/8oz	900g/2lb
sugar	200g/8oz	900g/2lb
eggs, at room temperature	6	24
almond essence	2–3 drops	1¼ teaspoons

Preheat the oven to 180C/350F/Gas 4. Grease the tin (or tins) required and line with baking parchment.

Arrange the cherries in the base of the tin. Sift the flour and salt together and mix in the ground almonds.

Beat the butter and sugar together until pale and fluffy. Beat the eggs and then add them to the butter and sugar mixture a little at a time, adding a spoonful of flour if the mixture shows signs of curdling. Add the almond essence. Fold in the flour and almond mixture.

Turn the mixture into the prepared tin. Bake in the oven for 1 hour or until the top feels springy to the touch and the cake is beginning to come away from the sides of the tin. Turn out, upside down, so that the base becomes the top of the cake, on to a cooling rack. **PG**

CHATSWORTH RICH FRUIT CAKE

This is one of the all-time best-sellers in the Farm Shop.

MAKES A 1.1KG/2½LB CAKE

grated zest and juice of 1 lemon
  and 1 orange
50ml/2fl oz brandy, plus
  1 tablespoon to finish
50g/2oz mixed peel
150g/5oz sultanas
150g/5oz raisins
150g/5oz currants
150g/5oz cherries
100g/4oz unsalted butter, at
  room temperature

3 medium free range eggs, at
  room temperature
50g/2oz melted butter for greasing
100g/4oz strong white flour
1 level teaspoon mixed spice
a pinch of ground ginger
a pinch of mace
25g/1oz ground almonds
25g/1oz flaked almonds
100g/4oz soft dark brown sugar

Mix the zest and juice of the orange and lemon with the 50ml/2fl oz of brandy, pour it over the dried fruit and leave to macerate overnight.

Preheat the oven to 140C/275F/Gas 1. Butter a 15cm/6in round cake tin, and line it with a double layer of greaseproof paper brushed with the melted butter.

Sift together the flour and spices and mix in the ground and flaked almonds.

In a separate large bowl, beat the sugar and unsalted butter together until pale and fluffy. Beat the eggs and add them a little at a time, adding a teaspoonful of the flour between additions if the mixture shows signs of curdling. Fold in the flour and almond mixture, and then add the brandied fruit. The mixture should be a soft, dropping consistency. Spoon it into the prepared tin, level the top, and bake for about 2 hours. It is ready when it feels springy to the touch and a metal skewer inserted into the centre of the cake comes out clean. Leave to cool in the tin, but place the tin on a rack.

Prick the top of the cake with a skewer and pour over the remaining tablespoon of brandy. Wrap the cake in foil and store in a cool, dry place. (We store our cakes for 6 months, to allow the flavour to improve slowly.) **AB**

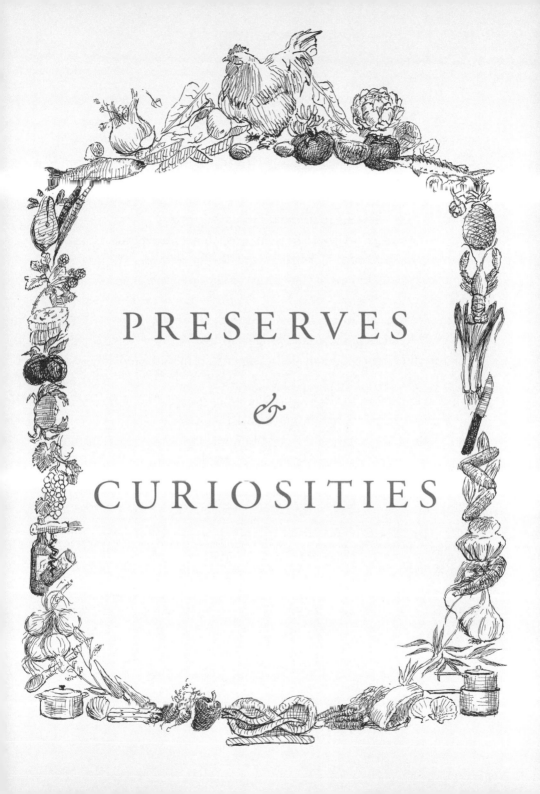

PRESERVES

&

CURIOSITIES

T HESE FAMILIARS OF OURS don't seem to fit any category, but I would be sorry not to include them, ranging as they do from spiced oranges to gull's eggs via jams and chutney and – my treat when the others are eating grouse, which I don't like – artichoke bottoms.

In the dark days of January there is the compensation of the arrival in the Farm Shop of Seville oranges and it's marmalade time again. All kinds of this breakfast necessity can be bought in shops in every combination of citrus fruit. Two, at least, have their devoted fans – Frank Cooper's Oxford Marmalade and Keiller's Dundee Marmalade. My father would only eat the latter and used to take it with him (and his own apples) on the rare occasions when he stayed in other people's houses. It was an insult to the hostess, no doubt, but my father preferred Keiller's Dundee Marmalade to her finer feelings. Fashion changes and it is no longer made in Dundee, so another prop of the past has disappeared.

But in spite of all the shops provide, none can rival home-made. The same goes for jam – why is it that, again, home-made is better? Is it the small scale of the making, the close attention to detail, or what? The best jam I have eaten for years is made by Nicholas Henderson, former ambassador to Paris and Washington. Whatever fruit he uses, you can happily eat it with a spoon and no bread. **DD**

OXFORD MARMALADE

We make marmalades from several different receipts, but the two I prefer are our attempt at copying Cooper's (the method was given to me by a native of Oxford, so I believe it is close to the real thing) and Bess's, whose origins are lost in the mists of time. They are different: Oxford is dark and stiff, Bess's is darker and runny – so, take your choice. **DD**

MAKES 10 X 350G/12OZ JARS

3kg/7lb Seville oranges, washed   caster sugar – see method below

Put the oranges in a pan and cover with water. Boil gently for 2–3 hours until they are tender. Take out the fruit, and reserve the liquid. Cut the oranges in half and take out the pips. Put the pips in a small basin, cover them with cold water and leave them to soak while slicing the oranges. Cut the oranges into strips, weigh them, and then place them in a preserving pan. For every 450g/1lb of fruit, add 700g/1lb 8oz of caster sugar and 275ml/½ pint of liquid taken from the water in which the oranges were boiled, plus the water in which the pips were soaked. Bring to the boil, turn down the heat, and simmer for about 2 hours.

Meanwhile, sterilise the jam jars by washing and rinsing them and then heating them in a moderate oven for 5 minutes. Turn off the oven but leave them in there so they are warm when you fill them with the hot marmalade. Put a couple of plates in the fridge to cool.

To test whether the marmalade will set, put half a teaspoonful on one of the cold plates, and cool in the fridge for a few moments. If a skin has formed and this wrinkles when you push with your finger, it is ready. If not, simmer for another few minutes. When it is ready, pour into the warm jars. Either place a waxed disc on top of the marmalade while it is still hot and seal with damp cellophane (packs of discs and cellophane and labels are available at stationers' shops) or wait until it is quite cold before capping.

If sealed properly and stored in a cool, dark place, the marmalade should keep for at least 2 years. **DW**

BESS'S MARMALADE

MAKES 16 X 350G/12OZ JARS

2.25kg/5lb Seville oranges, washed   **juice of 2 lemons**
3.6kg/8lb sugar

Cut the oranges in half and scoop out the pips and flesh into a colander, saving all the juice. Put the pips and flesh of the oranges into a square of muslin, tie tightly and put this into a large pan. Cut the oranges into quarters, slice them finely and add them to the pan. Pour in 4.5l/8 pints of water, adding any juice from the oranges. Bring to the boil and simmer gently for 2 hours.

When the orange peel is very tender, take it off the heat and add the sugar. Stir until all the sugar has dissolved. Put the pan back on the heat and simmer for another 2 hours or so.

For guidance on testing the marmalade for setting, and on sterilising and sealing the jars, and storing, see Oxford Marmalade, page 185. The only difference is that you should pour in the lemon juice when setting point has been reached, before you pot the marmalade. **HM**

STRAWBERRY JAM

MAKES 12 X 350G/12 OZ JARS

2kg/4lb 8oz fresh small strawberries   2kg/4lb 8oz preserving sugar
300ml/½ pint fresh lemon juice   with pectin

Rinse and hull the strawberries. Place in a non-metallic pan with the lemon juice and sugar and leave to macerate overnight.

Next day, slowly heat the mixture in a preserving pan, stirring gently to make sure all the sugar has dissolved. Turn up the heat to a full rolling boil. Boil for 10 minutes or until setting point is reached. If you have a sugar thermometer, this is when the temperature reaches 106C/220F. A better guide is the 'wrinkle' test: take the pan off the heat, place a small amount of syrup on a cold plate and put this in the fridge for a few moments to cool; if a skin forms and this wrinkles when you push with your finger, the jam is starting to set. If not, put it back on the heat to boil for another few minutes.

For guidance on sterilising and sealing jars, see Oxford Marmalade page 185. If sealed properly and stored in a cool, dark place, the jam should keep for a year, but once opened it will keep better if refrigerated. **AB**

BLACK CHERRY JAM WITH CHERRY BRANDY

MAKES 12 X 350G/12OZ JARS

2kg/4lb 8oz fresh or frozen dark
sweet cherries, stoned
300ml/½ pint fresh lemon juice

2.5kg/5lb 8oz preserving sugar
with pectin
125ml/4fl oz cherry brandy

If you are using fresh cherries, wash and halve them to remove the stones. Place in a preserving pan with 600ml/1 pint of water. Bring to the boil and simmer gently for about 10 minutes to soften the fruit. If you are using frozen cherries, the fruit will already be soft, so just add the liquid and heat gently.

Add the lemon juice and sugar and stir until the sugar has completely dissolved. Turn up the heat and bring to a full rolling boil. Boil for 10 minutes or until setting point is reached. If you have a sugar thermometer, this is when the temperature reaches 106C/220F. A better guide is the 'wrinkle' test: take the pan off the heat and place a small amount of syrup on a cold plate and put this in the fridge for a few moments to cool; if a skin forms and this wrinkles when you push with your finger, the jam is starting to set. If not, put it back on the heat to boil for another few minutes.

When it is ready, remove from the heat and add the cherry brandy.

For guidance on sterilising and sealing the jars, see Oxford Marmalade page 185.

If sealed properly and stored in a cool, dark place, this jam should keep for about 18 months, but once opened it will keep better if refrigerated. **AB**

LEMON CURD

MAKES 4 X 350G/12OZ JARS

175g/6oz butter
1kg/2lb 2oz granulated sugar
300ml/½ pint freshly squeezed
  lemon juice

grated zest of 4 unwaxed lemons
4 large free range eggs

Using a double saucepan, melt the butter. Add the sugar, lemon juice and zest, and stir until the sugar is completely dissolved. Beat the eggs well, add them to the sugar and lemon mixture, and continue to stir until the mixture thickens to the consistency of custard. While still hot, pour into thoroughly clean, dry, warm jars and cap.

For guidance on sterilising and sealing the jars, see Oxford Marmalade page 185.

If sealed properly and stored in a cool, dark place, the lemon curd will keep for up to a year, but once opened it should be refrigerated and eaten within 10 days. **AB**

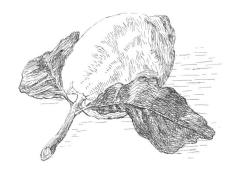

APRICOT AND WALNUT CHUTNEY

MAKES 12 X 350G/12OZ JARS

700g/1lb 8oz dried apricots

250g/9oz shelled walnuts

375g/13oz onions

700g/1lb 8oz apples, peeled and
  cored

250g/9oz sultanas

800g/1lb 12oz sugar

35g/1½oz mixed spice

a pinch of salt

600ml/1 pint cider vinegar

Chop the apricots and walnuts into quarters. Chop the onions and apples into 1cm/½in pieces. Place in a pan and add the remaining ingredients. Bring to the boil and simmer gently for about 1½ hours. If the chutney is still runny, turn up the heat to boil off the excess liquid. Allow to cool for 10 minutes. Pour into thoroughly clean, dry, warm jars. Cover with a waxed disc and cap.

For guidance on sterilising and sealing the jars, see Oxford Marmalade page 185.

If sealed properly and stored in a cool, dark place, the chutney should keep for a year. **AB**

CUMBERLAND SAUCE

This is a perfect accompaniment to hot or cold ham.

MAKES 4 X 350G/12OZ JARS

2 shallots, finely chopped

grated zest and juice of 3 oranges

grated zest and juice of 3 unwaxed
    lemons

2 heaped teaspoons arrowroot

250ml/9fl oz port or red wine

500g/1lb 2oz redcurrant jelly

flaked sea salt

freshly ground black pepper

Place the shallots in a small pan and just cover with water. Bring to the boil
and simmer until most of the liquid has evaporated and the shallots are soft
and moist.

Cook the orange and lemon zest in boiling water for 3–5 minutes. Drain,
and add to the shallots.

In a separate bowl, mix the arrowroot with a tablespoon of the port or
red wine until smooth.

To the shallots in the pan, add the redcurrant jelly, the remainder of the
port or wine, and the orange and lemon juice and bring to the boil. Remove
from the heat and slowly whisk in the arrowroot mixture. Return to the heat
and simmer for 1 minute. Season to taste.

While it is still hot, pour the sauce into thoroughly clean, dry, warm jars
and cap. It can be stored in a cool, dark place for up to a month. Once
opened it is best eaten straightaway. **AB**

CAREYSVILLE SPICY ORANGES

We try to emulate this unusual accompaniment to cold meat which originated in the kitchen at Careysville in Co. Cork. The Devonshires bought this square, grey, late Georgian house, built on a cliff overlooking the River Blackwater in 1947.

My father-in-law's reason for wanting the house was the mile and a half of fishing rights on both banks of the River Blackwater which went with it. Here is some of the best salmon fishing in Europe, the season running from 1 February to the end of September. Andrew and his father used to look forward to the opening day all the winter and the river seldom fails to produce wonderful sport. In a good year you can stand at the drawing-room window high above the fast-running stream and watch the fish, fresh from the sea, leaping out of the water, queuing 'in layers', as a ghillie used to say, for the 'fish pass' at the side of the weir to continue their journey up the river to spawn.

The whole day is spent by the water casting from the bank or from a shallow boat in mid-stream. There is a hut where, out of the wind and rain at last, long lunches are eaten and a fierce stove warms the frozen February fishermen. Till lately there was no road to the lunch hut and two people carried hampers containing the food down precipitous steps from the house and across a field, as if in a scene in a fairy story.

One reheated 'hot' dish and cold ham and beef, followed by fruit cake, are the traditional fare, which has never changed. It was to help the cold meat go down that this spicy orange was made by an inventive Careysville cook. DD

MAKES 2 X 1 LITRE/2 PINT KILNER JARS

12 small oranges	25g/1oz root ginger, grated
1.15k/2½lb caster sugar, washed	12 cloves
570ml/1 pint white wine vinegar	2 cinnamon sticks

1ST STAGE

Cut the oranges across the segments into slices about 5mm/¼in thick. Lay the slices in a large pan. Pour in 1.7l/3 pints of water. Cut out a disc of greaseproof paper the same diameter as the pan.

Bring the water in the pan to the boil, turn down the heat, cover the orange slices with the greaseproof paper and a lid, and simmer for 35–40 minutes until the peel is tender.

In another pan, slowly dissolve the sugar in the vinegar, add the spices and simmer for about 10 minutes. Drain the poaching liquid from the orange slices and set it aside. Being careful not to break the slices, transfer them into a large, non-metallic bowl and pour the vinegar mixture over them. Cover and leave in a cool place for 24 hours.

2ND STAGE

Return the orange slices, vinegar and spices to the large pan and add enough of the drained poaching liquid barely to cover the fruits. Keep the remaining liquid and use it to top up the oranges when they are simmering. Simmer very gently for 30–40 minutes until the orange peel looks slightly transparent. Return the orange slices and their liquor to the bowl and again leave for 24 hours.

3RD STAGE

Put 2 clean, dry Kilner jars to warm. Drain the liquor from the fruits and boil it rapidly until it is thick and syrupy. Discard the the spices. Return the orange slices to the syrup and heat very slowly to just below boiling point, and then take off the heat.

Arrange the orange slices neatly in the jars, pouring in a little of the syrup between layers. Cover and keep for at least 6 weeks (though the flavour continues to improve for up to a year as the spicy orange matures). HM

GULLS' EGGS

Gulls' eggs have the shortest season possible, which makes them all the more desirable. Even the all-powerful supermarkets have not found a way of producing gulls' eggs all the year round, so they remain a delicious sign of spring.

Large numbers of black-headed gulls nest on one area of the moor at Bolton Abbey. These gulls are not protected by law like plovers, for instance, but Ben Heyes, the land agent, has to get a licence from DEFRA to take eggs and the permitted number is limited. Whatever the weather or temperature, the gulls start laying on or about 26 April and the keepers pick up the eggs for the next eight to ten days. A game dealer buys them and sells them on to restaurants and hotels, where they are counted as a delicacy.

The gulls lay a clutch of three eggs in an apology for a nest, just a few rushes and stalks of dead grass pushed together on the ground. The male and female take it in turns to incubate them for twenty-three days when they hatch. To make sure a chick has not started to form, you must only take from a nest with a single egg in it. If there are two eggs, one could be fertile and if so, will be horrible when you come to shell it; and if there are three in the nest, leave well alone. Looking for eggs can be an un-nerving experience as these agile birds dive-bomb you, swooping down at speed, just missing your head. After the agreed number of eggs have been gathered, the birds are left in peace to incubate, hatch and rear their brood.

In early June the Bolton Abbey Estate takes local schoolchildren on trailers behind tractors up on the moor to learn from the keepers how heather moorland is managed for grouse. By this time the black-headed gull chicks have hatched and are running about. They are a great attraction for the children, some of whom are incredulous when the keepers explain that they have started life as an egg. It seems that there is a long way to go in education about the natural world. **DD**

Put the gulls' eggs into a pan of cold water, bring to the boil, and simmer for 20 minutes. Plunge them into cold water to cool quickly.

Shell the eggs and serve them with thin slices of brown bread and butter, celery salt and cayenne pepper.

CHEESE ICE

I bless Lady Sysonby for cheese ice. For a summer first course or a savoury you can't beat it, guaranteed as it is to surprise and please. Make sure to put lettuce or some other green leaves around the dish if offering it as a savoury lest the unsuspecting reckon it is vanilla ice cream. The shock of the taste of cheese when it looks like something sweet is like the shock of Marmite sandwiches to Americans, who expect Marmite to be a first cousin of marmalade.

Lady Sysonby's Cook Book of 1935 is a grander affair than Mrs Alhusen's. She persuaded Osbert Sitwell to write the introduction and Oliver Messel to make a few drawings. Osbert ended his piece 'to conclude, this book is for those not necessarily rich who want good food and mean to have it'. As you are often advised to add twenty slices of truffles, I am not sure what Osbert meant by 'rich' but Lady Sysonby does 'highly recommend English tinned green peas', so perhaps that equals out the truffles and many, liberal splashes of cognac. DD

SERVES 6

275ml/½ pint double cream
60g/2½ oz fresh and finely grated
  Parmesan
½ teaspoon flaked sea salt
freshly ground pepper to taste
1 teaspoon Tabasco sauce
a pinch of cayenne pepper

TO GARNISH
paprika for dusting
2 bunches of watercress
3 tablespoons pine kernels, toasted
  (optional)

Stir together the cream, Parmesan, salt, pepper, Tabasco and cayenne pepper. Pour into ice cube trays – preferably ones with holes big enough to hold 2 tablespoons of mixture. Freeze for at least 3 hours or until solid. Turn the cubes out as you would ice. Place on a cold serving dish and leave in the fridge for half an hour to soften them very slightly.

Serve dusted with a pinch of paprika and garnished with the watercress leaves and the pine kernels, if you use them. HM

INSTEAD-OF-GROUSE
ARTICHOKE BOTTOMS

What a waste, to live near grouse and say no to it. But I do, so while the others pull the birds to pieces, suck the bones and luxuriate in the fried breadcrumbs, bread sauce and gravy, I have an artichoke bottom (this is another unappetising English translation – 'fond' sounds better but is a bit precious). **DD**

This dish is like several that we serve at Chatsworth in that it looks complicated and involves various stages. But most of the work can be done ahead, and then reheated and assembled at the last moment. We sometimes replace the chicken liver sauce with a poached egg and Hollandaise sauce.

SERVES 6 AS A FIRST COURSE, OR 3 AS A MAIN COURSE

juice of 1½ lemons, plus ½ a cut
  lemon
6 x 300g/11oz artichokes
1 tablespoon flour
2 tablespoons olive oil
1 tablespoon salt
25g/1oz butter
flaked sea salt
freshly ground black pepper
½ tablespoon finely chopped parsley

FOR THE MUSHROOM PURÉE
25g/1oz butter
50g/2oz shallots, finely chopped
1 garlic clove, finely chopped
300g/11oz mushrooms, coarsely
  chopped
2 tablespoons double cream
1 tablespoon finely chopped parsley

FOR THE CHICKEN LIVER
SAUCE
450g/1lb chicken livers
570ml/1 pint milk
75g/3oz clarified butter
75g/3oz shallots, finely chopped
1 garlic clove, finely chopped
1 bay leaf
1 sprig fresh, or ½ teaspoon dried,
  thyme
100ml/4fl oz Madeira
275ml/½ pint brown chicken stock
  (see page 28)

Cut any green discolouration off the chicken livers and leave them to soak in the milk to 24 hours.

Half fill a non-metallic bowl with water, and acidulate it by adding the juice of half a lemon. Now trim the artichokes, one by one. First, snap off the stalk so that any fibres come off with it. Then, with a sharp stainless steel serrated knife, cut off a few of the bottom leaves and trim the base so it is flat. Starting from the base, pare away the layers of leaves, leaving only the fleshy leaf base, and continue until you have cleared about 2.5cm/1in. Then cut horizontally through the artichoke, discarding the top leafy part. Trim off any tough outer green patches, but do not try to scoop out the 'choke'. Rub the exposed artichoke flesh with the cut side of the ½ lemon to prevent it from discolouring. Place in the acidulated water. Repeat this process for all the artichokes.

Prepare the cooking liquor by whisking the flour with the olive oil and the juice of the remaining lemon and about 1.2l/2 pints of water in a pan that is big enough to hold the artichoke bottoms. Add a tablespoon of salt. Cut out a disc of greaseproof paper the same diameter as the saucepan. Bring the liquor to the boil, whisking from time to time. Be careful: this liquor boils over very easily. Add the drained artichoke bottoms and cover with the greaseproof paper. Simmer for 25–30 minutes until tender. Remove the artichokes from the liquor and leave them to drain, bases up, on a rack. When they are cool enough to handle, scoop out the furry 'chokes' with a teaspoon and discard these. Place the artichokes in a pan with a few tablespoons of cold water and the butter, ready to be reheated. Season with salt and pepper. Seal the pan with foil or cover with a lid.

Make the mushroom purée, following the instructions on page 86.

Start preparing the sauce by draining the chicken livers and cutting them into 1cm/½in dice. Melt the clarified butter in a frying pan over a high heat and cook half the livers until brown all over but pink inside. Transfer them into a saucepan. Repeat using the remaining livers. Season with salt and pepper and set aside. Add the shallots, garlic, thyme and bay leaf to the frying pan, and cook for 1–2 minutes to soften the vegetables. Add the Madeira and stock. Bring to the boil and boil until the liquid has been reduced by a third. Check the seasoning, and discard the sprig of thyme and the bay leaf.

Shortly before serving, turn on the heat beneath the artichokes, and reheat the mushroom purée and the sauce

Pour the sauce over the cooked chicken livers. Place the artichokes on a warm dish, fill each with mushroom purée and top with chicken livers sprinkled with the chopped parsley. **HM**

CIDER CUP

When Lady Astor reigned at Cliveden, in Buckinghamshire, she frowned on alcohol and lots of other things, being a crusading Christian Scientist. Her religious views didn't stop her from being the best company in the world, funny, quick as lightning, outrageous, small, pretty with glittering blue eyes, generous, kind and unkind, shocking and shocked. Her first marriage to an alcoholic, and her religion, set her on a lifelong campaign against drink. With her own extraordinary energy she did not need any extra stimulus and she did not allow that others might.

For some illogical reason cider cup flowed in her house. Perhaps Mr Lee, the butler, invented it for thirsty guests, as there was no wine at meals and neither were there spirits on the drinks tray. Whatever its origins, it deserves to be kept going.

I was lucky enough to go to Cliveden as a girl, as we lived at nearby High Wycombe. I went there in the first car that I owned, a second-hand Austin 7 which cost £14. It looked a bit odd parked by the Daimlers and Rolls-Royces of the other guests. Andrew's family had grown up with the Astors and he was friends, as I was, with the two younger boys, Michael and Jakie. The summer holidays found them all playing cricket and tennis at Cliveden, and a supremely jolly time was had by all.

The company was mixed. You never knew whom you might find yourself sitting next to at lunch. It was a bit unnerving for a seventeen-year-old girl, to find herself struggling to think of something to say to an American politician or a junior member of the Royal Family. Lady Astor was an entertainer and was never at a loss. Once some dreary man was droning on about his own subject when she stopped him with her Southern dropped g's: 'That's very interestin' – but I'm not interested.' And having shouted out some extraordinary statement, when questioned by her neighbour, she retorted, 'Well, how do I know what I think till I've heard what I said.'

It was always summer and hot at Cliveden, and this Cider Cup is a reminder of the happiest days there. **DD**

MAKES 8 GLASSES

2 x 330ml cans or 2 pints of ginger
  beer
660ml or 2 pints of medium cider

3 slices of orange
3 slices of lemon
sprigs of fresh mint

Mix in a large jug and serve chilled.

LADY GAGE'S DRINK
FOR ARTHRITIS AND RHEUMATISM

This is certainly a curiosity and also a mystery. It takes six weeks to work, according to Diana Gage (see page 81), who introduced it to this country from America. A friend has faithfully drunk it for the prescribed time. 'Has it worked?' 'Yes,' he said. I know a sample of one may not satisfy the medical profession, but it's a good start. **DD**

MAKES 2.25L/4 PINTS

3 grapefruits, washed

3 oranges, washed

3 lemons, washed

50g/2oz cream of tartar

50g/2oz Epsom salts

Cut the fruits into halves. Squeeze the juice from all the fruits and set aside. Remove the pith from the skins of the fruits using a soup spoon. Process all the skins, turn them out into a bowl and pour 1.2l/2 pints boiling water over them. Add the fruit juice, allow to cool, and leave to stand all night in the fridge. Next day, put the skins and juice, a little at a time, in a fine sieve or a sieve lined with a muslin cloth and extract as much juice as possible.

Now dissolve the cream of tartar and Epsom salts in 570ml/1 pint of boiling water and add to the juice. Pour the mixture into bottles – do not overfill – and keep cool. Shake the bottle well before taking, because the cream of tartar will settle at the bottom.

DOSE: take one wine glass before breakfast (but take only one dose daily). Keep taking it for a period of 22 weeks, by which time the system should have thrown off all the stiffness of the joints.

ICE RINGS

Wine that needs to be chilled stands in a ring of ice on our drinks tray. I stole the idea from Mark's Club, where surely all the best in London is found. Not only is everything you eat there superb, but instead of a hard restaurant chair you sink into an enveloping sofa exactly right for comfort, and the surrounding pictures of dogs and cows make you happy before you start. Proper food is on the menu – ham, bread-and-butter pudding, and a bitter chocolate ice which defies description.

The ice ring is just another perfectionist detail of Mark Birley's. It is easy to make – which I know that the apparently simple food of the calibre that is served there is not. **DD**

Stand an empty wine or champagne bottle in the centre of a 2l/3½ pint pan or a straight-sided jug and fill the pan or jug with cold water. Make sure that you release any trapped air bubbles from the bottom of the bottle. (You can add ice cubes, flower petals, herbs or leaves to the water before freezing to add to the visual effect.) Freeze until solid.

To free the ring, fill the bottle with warm water to loosen it, and then remove the bottle. Invert the pan under a running warm tap and gently ease the ring from the pan.

To serve, put the ring into a chilled glass bowl to catch the water as the ice melts, and insert the full bottle of wine or champagne to be chilled.

INDEX

AUTHOR'S ACKNOWLEDGEMENTS

I would like to thank the people who have done all the work for this book.
They are:

Hervé Marchand, the chef at Chatsworth,
and Darren Wright, his assistant,
who have cooked everything;
André Birkett, General Team Manager at the Farm Shop,
Paul Neale, Head Butcher,
and Christine Burns, André's Administrative Assistant;
Philip Gates, Head of Catering in the Carriage House Restaurant,
Paul Cotterell, Head Chef, Amanda Harrison, Head Baker,
and Anne Thompson and Margaret Brightmore, Philip's secretaries.

I am grateful to the people who have allowed me to use their receipts:
Mark Birley, Margaret Budd, Lord Gage, Nicky Haslam,
Candida Lycett-Green and Kathleen Penny.

Will Topley has drawn people, places and food.
Anne Wilson has jig-sawed words and pictures into shape.
Tristram Holland has sat for many hours in Midland Mainline trains
to and from Chesterfield in aid of editing and much-needed help.
Helen Marchant has really written the book, although she is meant
to look after Andrew and a good deal else.

My grateful thanks are due to all these extraordinary people –
without whom the kitchens would not be the same and there would
be no receipt book.

DD